religiously **transmitted** diseases

religiously **transmitted** diseases

by Ed Gungor

NELSON BOOKS
A Division of Thomas Nelson Publishers
Since 1798

www.thomasnelson.com

Nelson Books titles may be purchased in bulk for educational, fundraising or sales promotional use. For information, please e-mail SpecialMarkets@ThomasNelson.com.

Unless otherwise indicated, Scriptures are taken from the HOLY BIBLE, NEW INTERNATIONAL VERSION®. Copyright © 1973, 1978, 1984 by International Bible Society. Used by permission of Zondervan Publishing House.

Other versions used:

The New King James Version (NKJV). Copyright © 1982 by Thomas Nelson, Inc. Used by permission. All rights reserved.

The King James Version of the Bible (KJV).

The Living Bible (TLB), copyright © 1971 by Tyndale House Publishers, Wheaton, IL. Used by permission.

The Message (MSG), copyright © 1993. Used by permission of NavPress Publishing Group.

New American Standard Bible (NASB), © 1960, 1977 by the Lockman Foundation. Used by permission.

The Contemporary English Version (CEV) © 1991 by the American Bible Society. Used by permission.

The *International Children's Bible* (ICB)®, *New Century Version*®, copyright © 1986, 1988, 1999 by Tommy Nelson®, a Division of Thomas Nelson, Inc. Used by Permission.

The Amplified Bible: Old Testament. Copyright © 1962, 1964 by Zondervan Publishing House (used by permission); and The Amplified New Testament. Copyright © 1958 by The Lockman Foundation (used by permission) (www.Lockman.org).

The *Holy Bible*, New Living Translation (NLT), copyright © 1996. Used by permission of Tyndale House Publishers, Inc. Wheaton, Illinois 60189. All rights reserved.

New Life Version (NLV) Copyright © 1969 by Christian Literature International.

The New Testament: A Translation in Modern English for Today's Reader by Olaf M. Norlie (NOR), © 1961 by Zondervan Publishing House.

The WeymouthTranslation

Library of Congress Cataloging-in-Publication Data

Gungor, Ed.
    Religiously transmitted diseases / by Ed Gungor.
      p. cm.
    Includes bibliographical references.
    ISBN 1-59951-001-4
  1. Christian life. I. Title.
  BV4501.3.G86 2006
  248.4—dc22

                                              2006006980

Printed in the United States of America
06 07 08 09 10 RRD 6 5 4 3 2

To the love of my life and the girl from
my childhood dreams, Gail Gungor.

With my wife/best friend of more than thirty years, we have witnessed both the best and the worst of times, together. And she helps me remember what *really* happened. She is, for me, the goodness of God wrapped up in one spot.

You still make my heart skip, girl. Thank you for holding on to us.
—Edwin

He who finds a wife finds a good thing.
Proverbs 18:22 NKJV

contents

contents

preface: first thoughts

"I have herpes," she blurted out, as tears streamed down her face.

I was stunned. I had watched Sarah grow up. She was beautiful. Smart. A college grad. She had great parents, rather strict, but they tipped the scale in her favor more often than not. As she told her story, it was clear that, in spite of her fairly restrictive upbringing, once she got the freedom college afforded, it wasn't checked with wisdom.

"I don't know what I was thinking," she muttered. "I started hanging out with people who loved to party, and I started drinking a little to fit in."

The "big party" had promised free alcohol and cute boys. After a few drinks, one of these "hotties" started hitting on her. One thing led to another, and before she could grasp the gravity of it, they were having sex. They only did it one time—her *first* time—but she contracted incurable herpes.

She had lived with her dark secret, telling no one, for more than three years. Now she was telling me, only because she had fallen in love with Sam, a great professional guy in our church (who was a virgin), and he had popped the marriage question. But she hadn't told him about the herpes.

"I need to tell him," she said.

"Yeah, you do," I responded, and we talked a little about the where, when, and how of approaching him with it. Then I prayed with her, holding a dim hope that Sam might be OK with it.

But Sam wasn't OK with it. It wasn't that he didn't love her; he did. He just didn't want to deal with all the complexity a sexually transmitted disease brings to a relationship. Their wonderful relationship ended. It was destroyed.

Disease does that. It destroys things—things that were once wonderful.

Like faith . . .

introduction

These are the ramblings of a guy who has been a follower of Jesus for more than thirty-five years. I'm not exactly an old guy, but I can see "old" pretty clearly from here.

It has been my experience that in religious life, I tend to get it wrong more than I get it right, but God seems to put up with it. Apparently, who we are is more important to Him than what we do.

My wife, Gail, and I have four children. As far as family life is concerned, our kids also routinely tended to get it wrong. Beds went unmade, shoes were left in the hall, and there was a failure to heed all the *don'ts* and *stop its* and *come heres*. But we put up with it. We, too, were more taken with who Michael and Robert and David and Elisabeth were, than with what they did or didn't do. Maybe we got that from God.

I want to have a conversation with you about what I think goes wrong in faith, about how things get weird, even diseased. I hope to provoke you to conduct a spiritual "checkup."

I remember the hour I first believed. It was sweet. It was innocent. It was charged with life and hope. I don't think God ever intended for that to change. Yet, for many, it has. I want to talk about why I think that is true. Some will not agree with my assessments, but that's OK. I simply want to stir you up to ask more questions and tout fewer answers that, more often than not, are really just empty platitudes.

I wish this were a face-to-face chat. Often, words alone sound so short and harsh—especially when controversial issues are being discussed. I prefer the way facial expressions and tone of voice aid the communication process. But all I have are words, so I have labored long over this writing in the hope of softening my tone. I want to speak kindly to God's family. But if I step on your toes too hard, please forgive me and know that I tried to take my shoes off first.

1

unreligion: recapturing the romance

I think Christianity is supposed to be the *un*religion. That's because the strictness and predictability of religion causes simple, pure faith to become diseased. If not stopped, religion can even kill living faith. And dead things just aren't very interesting. Case in point . . .

I was eleven years old the first time I dissected anything. I was on a scouting trip. Armed with flashlights, a few of us wandered into the woods after dark to explore.

Joe was the first to spot him. He was a pretty good-sized frog. And he was quick. Flashlights and size-8 feet darted every which way as we scrambled to grab him. Something in us boys wanted to know what was inside that frog, what made that living thing *alive*.

"Don't kill it!" Joe cried. "Take him alive."

I'm sure that frog had no idea he was going to stumble into the midst of a gaggle of earth giants that night, and he did his best to flee, but to no avail. I got my hand around him as he tried to hop between my feet. Then we each whipped out our scout-issued jackknives and begged to be the surgeon.

In a few moments, the frog lay dead, his inner secrets uncovered. But to my surprise we didn't gain any greater understanding of Froggie when we opened him up. We had lost something. The interest that had charged the air during the hunt completely disappeared

1

when he lay open and lifeless before us. Dead things aren't nearly as attention-grabbing as things that are alive. Only in the presence of life does mystery exist.

My quest to dissect continues to this day. It is as though I am uncomfortable with wonder. I find something full of life and, instead of enjoying the mystery of it, I want to dissect it, to figure out the how and why. But dissecting life results in death. And once death comes, the mystery disappears.

Religion, too, is all about dissecting. It is the nemesis of mystery.

But religion does have its attraction. It is so neat, so organized, so repetitive, so habitual, and oh-so-predictable. It makes God look more like a clock than a person—ticking and tocking in a perfectly ordered way. Life isn't nearly so conventional. It is messy and full of surprises. Repetitious? Yes, but certainly not predictable.

I have conducted more funerals this year than in recent memory. We often say that dead people "rest in peace." I think we are fooled by the way they just lie there. No complaining. No whining. Just nice and stiff and orderly—religious, really. That's because religion is *anti*life in some ways. It demands order and fixation, just as rigor mortis demands of the dead.

Religion may be attractive on one level, but it always strives to remove all the mystery that congests life. It has answers for everything, because questions are way too untidy. "Jesus is the answer." Right? But what if Jesus *isn't* the answer? What if He is the question?

MYSTERIOUS THINGS

As a kid, I always felt unfinished. I was unsettled, and something in my soul was in search mode. My mind and body were always in motion. There was an inner grinding that didn't stop from the moment I got up until I drifted off to sleep at night. I felt hungry.

2

Incomplete. Searching for a *where* or a *what* or a *why* everywhere I went.

My older brother Mark seemed to float through life. He was good at sports, made friends easily, and lived in the spotlight. I was fourteen months his junior and didn't fare nearly as well. I didn't float through life; I was towed. I would make friends, bring them home, and then Mark would take it from there. I would try out for sports, but due to a pretty stiff case of childhood asthma, and no coaching, I was the last one to get picked for teams.

"You take Gungor," one captain would say to the other.

"No way. I had him last time," was the retort. "I'll take the fat girl."

Then there was God. I didn't know quite what to make of God. I grew up in a traditional, liturgical church that left a lot of information about God in the dark. After all, God wasn't the issue; we were. Faith was all about how we performed. But no worries; as long as you covered the basics (church attendance, participation in the sacraments, etc.), you could count on God understanding where you were. And though He was a very busy and mysterious Deity, you had a fair shot at staying in His good graces and getting into heaven.

But I fell in love with God in that church, as much as I knew of Him. I guess I loved the idea of mystery and the reverence inspired by it. I also loved the statues and the symbolism. I even became an altar boy. Some Sundays I would go to two services just to try to be closer to this mysterious Being. But then adolescence kicked in, with all its fury. I abandoned my journey to discover the mystery surrounding God to investigate a new mystery: *girls.*

SALVATION

It was Christmas 1970 when my best friend told me he had just "given his life to Jesus" and said I should do the same. I pretended to know what he meant but really didn't. How do you give your life to someone? And if I could answer that, would Jesus even *want* whatever that meant? But the idea stuck with me. *Give your life to Jesus.*

Something in me always wanted to belong. If I ran into someone I thought was cool or enviable, I would try to be like him or her. At best, I was open to changing my life. At worst, I became most like the person I was last with. I certainly was not centered, but I definitely leaned toward the spiritual side of things.

One time I met a guy who was carrying a Bible around. He was really cool, so I checked out the *one* Bible in my school library and carried it around with me for six months. I tried to read it a little but got to the Old Testament dietary laws and lost interest. (A love for bacon had something to do with that.)

But Christmas 1970 was a different deal.

I was at a dance when my friend Nick told me I should give my life to Jesus. I had purchased some pot and was trying to keep a buzz going long into the night. I had just smoked some before arriving home around two in the morning., but all I could think was, *Ed, give your life to Jesus.* Suddenly, as I climbed the stairs to my room, I turned stone-cold sober. Believe me when I say, *that* was weird.

When I walked into the room, something was there. It wasn't exactly like the presence of another person. It was bigger. And it wasn't scary, but it demanded awe. Somehow I knew it was God.

I remember literally falling to my knees by my bed and calling on Mary and Joseph (and a couple other saints I could think of), as well as Jesus. I felt like a sinner, which was bizarre. I had always thought God understood my true intentions to be good and would overlook my faults. But in this moment, I felt dirty—not because He was making me feel that way, but because I *was*. Yet I also felt totally accepted.

The next few days were wonderful. I became an utter God-lover. When I looked around, everything seemed different. I felt so alive, and I had no fear of death. If anything, the thought of death made me smile. *I'd get to see Jesus,* I mused. God Almighty had chosen to live in my heart, so I loved everything and everybody: my teachers, my parents, the pope, the police, the trees and birds, *everything.*

Later I discovered that I had experienced what Jesus called being "born-again." Many try to reduce this experience to some kind of religious drama or routine: (1) come forward in a meeting; (2) pray this prayer; (3) say these words; (4) believe these Bible verses; and *presto,* you will be saved. I know some people have spiritual encounters that way (though I would argue that the moment is actually a culmination of a whole complex series of events orchestrated previously by God). I also know of many churches that boast of thousands coming to Christ in response to altar calls. Yet these churches have a hard time drawing even a fraction of those "thousands" into the life of the church. I'm just not sure the "instant conversion tactic" works as well as church leaders think. I'm not sure God ever intended for us to force encounters with Him into the rigor mortis of a religious pattern.

God met me while I was calling on Mary, Joseph, the saints—and Jesus—and *not* using the words on the back of the how-to-be-saved tract. I may have done it wrong, but I met God.

SWEET MYSTERY

On our fifteenth wedding anniversary, I told Gail to pack enough clothes for four days. I arranged everything in advance: the babysitting, the travel arrangements, the hotels, and the tickets for the events we were to attend. She knew nothing about my plans.

"Where are we going?" she asked.

"I'm not telling," I responded.

After bludgeoning me with questions for a couple of days, she gave up trying to unearth my secret plan. I knew she was excited, and *not* knowing seemed to provoke anticipation in her. The night before we were to leave, I surprised her with the early arrival of the sitter. I told her to grab her stuff—right now—and jump in the car. She smiled and instantly complied (it's amazing how easily women submit to love).

We traveled for a few hours, stayed in a cozy inn, and got up early the next morning. We then drove about two miles to the train station. She still had no idea where we were headed.

We boarded the Amtrak bound for Illinois and enjoyed a snowy, Dr. Zhivagoesque ride from central Wisconsin to Union Station in Chicago. We then cabbed to a lovely hotel with a fireplace and fifteen red roses waiting. The next four days were filled with pre-planned dinners, plays, concerts, and shopping.

Gail had no knowledge of what we were going to do until I told her to get ready. But she enjoyed the mystery. And instead of nagging me daily with questions, she just sat back and experienced the moment. She said the mystery was "romantic."

I think we long for romance because God is romantic. I also believe there is to be romance and mystery in our journey of faith. The apostle Paul penned, "Now to him who is able to do immeasurably more than all we ask or imagine . . ." (Eph. 3:20). I think a huge part of why we get religious diseases is that we try to avoid all the mystery inherent in faith. We try to systematize everything surrounding faith: our beliefs, our experiences, our outcomes—we want control over everything we have and everyone we know. We no more appreciate mystery than we do appendicitis.

I've been on this journey of faith for a long time. In that time, I've found that many things happen to us, and to those around us, that we can't figure out. We need to learn to be OK with not knowing exactly what is going on.

I'm not saying you shouldn't try to figure it out, but after you try and still come up empty, smile—chill. Be OK with God's being romantically in charge. Be OK with *questions.*

6

The Greek Orthodox Church speaks of *apophatic* theology, a theology that celebrates what we *don't* know about faith and about God. Paul said it this way: "Oh, the depth of the riches of the wisdom and knowledge of God! How unsearchable his judgments, and his paths beyond tracing out!" (Rom. 11:33). Ah, sweet mystery. It keeps marriages alive and faith healthy. But beware. Religion tries to abort it. I think that's why the apostle John wrote, "Whoever has the Son, has life" (1 John 5:12 MSG). He doesn't mention religion.

2

borg disease: resistance is futile

Fitting in is killing me," Halley wailed. It was obvious she was frustrated.

Halley was a twenty-something, single registered nurse who had given her life to Christ during her college years. She was smart, well-spoken, and stylish.

"What do you mean by 'fitting in'?" I asked, certain that I knew exactly what she meant.

"When I first came to church here," she began, "I loved how people would talk with me and encourage me in my faith. I felt a gentle accountability that caused me to grow spiritually. But about a month ago I ran into this group that seemed more invasive than encouraging to me. They are very nice, but they have kind of inter-rogated me about everything I do, from what I wear to how I vote and what music I listen to. It's not that they're judgmental, but it's obvious that if I don't buy into their predetermined set of values, they think I am on dangerous ground—that I am not pleasing to God, or something.

"Please don't misunderstand me," she continued. "I want to be holy. I want Jesus Christ to be my Lord. But does that mean I have to wear outdated clothes and stop listening to Coldplay or other groups that don't have overtly Christian lyrics? Do I have to act just like those folks prescribe or be unpleasing to God? I mean, they all act the same, dress the same, respond the same—they remind me of a clique from high school."

I knew exactly the kind of group Halley was talking about. They are in every church: those wonderful believers who feel it is their job to play God and try to make others in *their* own likeness and image. They are Borgish.

THE BORG

I know it's no longer cool, but I'm a Trekkie, and I remember when the writers of the *Star Trek* TV series created a scary race of beings known as the Borg. They called themselves "the Collective," because each had relinquished his or her individuality to function as *one*.

The Borg was a pretty evangelistic group, because they assimilated everyone they bumped into along their way in the universe into the Collective. You could try to resist their invitation, but they simply replied, "Resistance is futile," and assimilated you anyway by infecting you with a self-duplicating, viruslike "nanoprobe" that changed you into Borg. All members of the Borg wore the same kind of clothing, walked and talked the same robotic way, and had all the trimmings one would expect to see in a horror show. Once you became Borg, there was no turning back.

Unfortunately, I have seen many groups inside churches and Christian ministries that were Borgish. These are not horrible people; in fact, they are often very kind and godly. But they are infected. They think they have everything figured out; hence, everyone else must look and act the same way.

In a Borg-infected group you will not see much individual expression. Not on your life. There is a predetermined set of mannerisms that are considered holy and right. These mannerisms usually come from Bible verses taken out of context or from deductions the leaders have made—deductions often based on biases against anything cool (or against women).

It's not unusual for these groups to wear out-of-style clothing (it takes about five to eight years for clothing styles to become "sanctified"), to display the same walk (modes of behavior), and to talk the same robotic way (codified "holy language" is held as a premium). If you value diversity and individuality, they are definitely a horror show.

We evangelicals are pretty susceptible to Borg disease, because many believe the weightier part of being a Christian has to do with external characteristics: what we wear, how we talk, what we like or dislike, and what we don't do. Let's face it: there is a Borgish, cookie-cutter culture that is touted in many Christian circles as "Christlike."

BE LIKE MIKE

After we first moved to the Tulsa area, our two oldest sons, Michael and Robert, attended a rather large Christian high school. Though Michael and Robert are both great kids, Michael fared the best. In fact, after being in school just a few months, he began to be showcased and honored. He was often publicly praised, received numerous awards, and ended up the homecoming king at the end of his first year. Of course, Gail and I believed he was an awesome kid, but something about the school's rush to celebration seemed a little disingenuous and a bit over the top.

Robert, on the other hand, kept getting the short end of the stick. At times the actions of both teachers and administration toward him were nothing short of unfair.

Initially we were confused about this seeming disparity until we realized that many of the educators in this Christian school system had an image in mind of what the perfect Christian student should be like. It just so happened that Michael fit the bill quite well. He is by nature outwardly compliant, nonconfrontational, and quiet. Consequently, he came across as exceptionally mature for his age. When they saw the traits they had been trying to cultivate in the other children *already* present in him, they quickly placed him on a pedestal.

Robert, conversely, opened his mouth too much. Though he was talented, an honor student, and loved God with a tender heart, he would challenge rules, point out hypocrisies, and generally push the envelope—he colored his hair, yelled and applauded in public assemblies to the point of overkill, etc. Robert was always just a little "out there."

If the school had taken time to really get to know Michael, they would have discovered that his perception of some of the rules was no different from that of any other teen: they were silly and nonessential. He was, in fact, just as opinionated and put-out as Robert over the hypocrisies he saw. He just preferred to leave things alone.

I'm not trying to take anything away from Michael, but my point is, *he was just being Michael.* He wasn't trying to appease and brownnose the teaching staff in hopes of becoming their poster child. Michael has enough integrity that if "being Michael" would have gotten him into trouble, he would still have been Michael and gotten into trouble.

As Robert and I watched this unfold, I said, "Robert, don't feel bad about all the attention Michael is getting or about how unfairly you are being scrutinized. You are just too different in personality to win in this school system. I wouldn't have won either. Michael is just being himself, and they like that—he is not compromising himself. For you to act like him would be a compromise. I could give you a crash course in brown-nosing so you could pretend to be something you are not, but that would be a tragedy. The truth is, I love your edginess. Though you could use a little more wisdom, please continue to be yourself—even if you scare some folks who don't get the idea of individuality. You may never get noticed as much as Michael, but that is OK with your mom and me. We are proud of both of you."

But many Christian leaders and educators believe that sameness *is* godliness, and they frown on variation. They are *Borg*.

BORG-FREE

We all want to be discipled into a pure form of Christianity, not some-one's *brand* of Christianity. And we want to be accountable to true godliness, not a human kind. But because most of us want to *belong* (not to belong brings terror), it is easy to just give in and try to meet the expectations of others. The problem is, we ultimately lose when we do that.

Paul wrote that we are all different, like the parts of the human body (1 Cor. 12:17), and he challenged each member to dare to be different—not to act and think the exact same way. Yes, we are *all* sup-posed to be holy. Yes, we are *all* supposed to be moral. Yes, we are *all* supposed to live ethically. But we are each to live out our holiness in the way we are wired: our different gifts, passions, and personalities.

Some of us may be more fashionable than others, some more conservative, some more edgy. Some of us are quiet, some more bombastic. Some are tattoo-friendly, others tattoophobic. It was the apostle Paul who said, "I have become all things to all men so that by all possible means I might save some" (1 Cor. 9:22). Maybe as we all express ourselves in ways that are congruent with our talents, passions, and personalities, we are best positioned to "save some"—because those "some" can relate to us.

Christianity is not supposed to be a retread Eastern mysticism that forces people to forfeit their distinctiveness as they are absorbed into some great cosmic oneness or sameness.

But *sameness* makes it easier for us to tell who the *insiders* are. Just as black leather and a Harley-Davidson are the marks of a biker; and tight jeans, western boots, and a huge silver belt buckle are the marks of a cowboy, certain other external attributes are fancied by some Christians as *the* marks of Christlikeness. Actually, it is easier to make Christianity about externals and man-made rules. But the downside is, unless you already "fit" the predetermined collection of personality traits set by the Christian culture to which you belong, you will be pressured to be something you are not. Christianity will feel restrictive and hold little joy for you. Satan loves that. He wants us all confused about what real Christianity is so that we live in some kind of synthetic, kissing-up belief system that is powerless.

Real apprentices of Jesus celebrate individual expression—that's the thing that best kills the Borg weirdness. Borg is about the *Collective*, about all being alike. It's about squashing individuality and uniqueness; it's about control. That's why Christian leaders are so predisposed to catching this disease—it promises them control.

But control is not leadership. To keep leadership clean from this disease, we must be willing to lose control. We must dare to respect people and to trust God. That would allow the saints of God to break into freedom—to dare to be diverse. Maybe that's the kind of freedom Malachi predicted would come to pass one day: "And you will go out and leap like calves released from the stall" (Mal. 4:2).

Maybe it's time to go leaping.

3

the deadly *o*: God is not for sale

There was no way I was going to make it in traditional evangelical Christianity. I was never good enough. Certainly never consistent enough. It was a willpower thing, and I never had much of it.

I wasn't *trying* to be wishy-washy. In fact, I longed for the kind of marine-sergeant iron will I saw in others. But my capacity for commitment was tragically flawed. For example, I would make a resolution to lose weight, deciding I wasn't going to eat any more pie. But I like pie. So, in spite of my *antipie* commitment, if I was offered pie (which seemed to occur with supernatural consistency after I made such commitments), my "no pie" resolution dissolved into an "only one piece" resolution. This led to the "only one *more* piece" resolution, which then carried me until no more pie existed.

In the church circles I grew up in, there was a lot of chatter about "commitment." In fact, *most* of the preaching I heard was about commitment. "If Jesus died for us, we must decide to live for Him" was the touted credo.

One night an old traveling preacher told a story that put the nail in the proverbial coffin for me.

"When I was a teenager," he began with his heavy Texas drawl, "we all used to drink Cokey-Colas. They were a nickel back then.

"I remember walking up to one of those Cokey-Cola machines

and reachin' into my pocket, searchin' for a nickel. I did it out of habit!" he declared with a note of disgust.

"I stopped and thought, *I'm not going to let this Cokey-Cola dominate me.* I looked at that machine and declared, 'I'll never drink another Cokey-Cola the longest day I live.' And praise God," he rumbled, shaking his jowls, "I never have."

I sat nonplussed. *I'm never going to make it,* was my first thought. I didn't have much willpower. But I had *lots* of passion—I was passionate for God one minute, passionate for sin the next! So, in a religious world, where spirituality was more about performance than desperation for God, things didn't look bright for me. I kept hoping there was something I could do that would "fix" me. The preachers said sticking to commitments and doing what was right were the keys to being a successful Christian. And I longed to do that.

A WATERSHED MOMENT

It was a summer night in our little Pentecostal church when the missionary-evangelist made the strongest appeal I had ever heard for a no-holds-barred, no-nonsense commitment to Jesus Christ. I had been in dozens of these altar calls before and had responded to them all. But the urgency was palpable. This guy grabbed my heart.

"This is what our young people need," he said in earnest, nearly in tears. "Commitment!"

He's right, I thought. And I joined the herd and went off to the altar to do business with God. At first, I was doubtful that this new commitment would really mean anything. As a teen, I had spent hundreds of hours at altars, trying to hit the mother of all commitments—the commitment of commitments that would keep me consistently holy. When I think back at how I acted at those altars, I probably looked a lot like a professional wrestler in the WWF, preparing for a match—huffing and puffing; slinging spit; waving my arms; and trying to convince myself that I was bigger, stronger, and able to "whup" whatever came into my "ring" of life.

But those jacked-up promises to God never lasted. Sure, they started out hopeful, but my commitments were like the squint you have when you walk out of a movie matinee on a sunny afternoon— you have a pretty good squint going at first, but it quickly wears off. I would come off those altars squinting like a pro. But after a few hours, or by the next morning, the squint wore off and I was back to my old tricks. Believe me, I was not happy about this. I was horrified when I realized I was more of a chameleon than a disciple. At church, I was holy. Home alone, I was not. I lived out my Christianity like the measles—I had faith, in spots. I even considered whether or not my inconsistency was caused by demons—maybe I could have someone cast them out of me?

As I knelt at that old, familiar altar that hot summer night, I felt nothing. No passion. No tears. No magic. I was face-to-face with the revelation that commitment was essential to the Christian experi- ence—and I was commitment challenged. I felt dead. Lost. It seemed as if that thing in us that *commits*—our "committer"—sort of fell out of my soul, landed on the altar, went into convulsions, and died. And though I was only about seventeen, my committer looked shriveled, charred, and about ninety-nine years old—I had used it that much. At that moment, I knew I would never be able to pull off this thing we call Christianity.

My only hope is to go to church a lot. Maybe Jesus will come back dur- ing a service; then I will be safe.

But at that dark moment, a verse came to mind. It was something Jesus said: "If a man remains in me and I in him, he will bear much fruit; apart from me you can do nothing" (John 15:5).

A light came on.

This verse was saying that being fruitless, doing "nothing," is *par* for a human being—apart from Jesus, that is. In other words, "nothing" is what God expects from fallen people who haven't yet learned how to rely on the grace of God.

It hit me—God had *never* expected us to perform for Him in our own strength—though I had always thought He had. I can't describe the hope and joy that exploded in me as I saw that our responsibility as believers was simply to come to Him, to "remain" in Him, to find ways to connect with Him, which would naturally result in our bearing "much fruit"—fruit that we are unable to bear on our own.

This was a watershed moment in my thinking about faith. I began to realize that the whole "commitment" thing that I was trying for years to perfect was misdirected. It was a hoax. Without realizing it, I had added an *o* to *God* in my life. I had made faith about "good"—my human good—instead of about *God*. But God was really after my commitment to *trust* Him, not my commitment to *perform* for Him. He wanted me to be committed to discovering how trust worked for a guy like me—with my personality and background. He never wanted me to jump through hoops for Him.

I don't know why it happens so easily, but most of us end up shifting the footing of our faith from God and His working in our lives to our own performance. But it doesn't make sense to trust ourselves. The only reason we are even open to faith in Jesus is because we are "taught by God" (John 6:45) to come to Him. This whole thing started with God. Faith itself is a gift (Eph. 2:8) *from* God. Though good always ends up emerging in a person who relies on Jesus, Christianity isn't about humans deciding to be good. The good we come up with on our own isn't really good anyway—it is like "filthy rags" (Isa. 64:6) in God's sight, always sullied with some hidden agenda.

Faith and discipleship were never supposed to be about committing to do *good*; it was to be about committing to *God*—the One who does good things *in* us. We can't produce Christianity. It is

17

supernatural. A promise at the altar to "be good" means about as much to God as promising to fly for Him. He knows we can't fly.

ONLY SUPERMAN CAN FLY

Only Superman can fly. But Lois had to discover that on her own.

In the second Superman movie that came out in the 1980s, Superman took Lois Lane flying with him. Early in the scene, Lois clung tightly to Superman, refusing even to look down. But as they flew around for a while, she became more and more confident. Slowly, she stopped clinging so desperately to Superman and began to stretch out her own arms, imitating him and pretending she could fly. Soon she forgot that her flight was only possible because of her connection to Superman. She inched out to the tips of his fingers, and then, *suddenly*, she lost connection and dropped like a stone! Superman swooped to catch her, and the meaning is clear: *only Superman can fly*.

In the arena of faith, only the God-man, Jesus, can fly. People can't. There is no way humans will ever be able to pull off divine goodness. That stuff is from another world. True, if you get up real high (really, really, really try to live right) and jump, you will have the illusion of flight, but it doesn't end well.

Discipleship is not about teaching people how to fly. Discipleship is about teaching people how to stay connected with Jesus, the only real Superman who ever lived. We have to fight not to make faith about *self*.

BEGINNINGS

In his science-fiction novel *Perelandra*, C. S. Lewis provides great insight into what occurred in the fall of humankind in Genesis 3.

Lewis depicts the lives of a man and woman living on another planet untainted by evil. He portrays the devil as a tempter, who comes to the woman and provides her with a mirror so she can reflect upon herself. It is in this *self-reflection* that evil is born.

Whenever we make faith about self, we miss the mark. Acting *for* God was never part of the program. God never created people to be performers—acting independently of a direct connection with Him—any more than manufacturers create appliances to work independently of a power source. We believe a lie when we think God is asking us to perform. It is also a lie that we can act perfect and take care of ourselves. Humans need God—we were created that way. Though good is the fruit of a life well connected with God, it is not the thing that gives us a connection with God.

There is grave danger in preaching a message of human performance. Such a sermon contends that there is something we can do to procure God's presence and favor in our lives. Doing good things somehow *earns* God. The problem is, God is not for sale. He only *gives* Himself to us.

The apostle Paul says it best. He said Christianity starts *from* God, it only works *through* God, and it ends up going back *to* God: "For from him and through him and to him are all things. To him be the glory forever!" (Rom. 11:36).

This isn't about good; this is about God. So drop the extra *o*. It's deadly to real faith.

inferiorphobia: bigger is always better

It was Narcissus, the ancient Greek son of the gods, who stumbled upon his own image at a pool of water and fell in love with what he saw. Legend has it that he was so awestruck that he couldn't pull away, and he died there, admiring himself. It is from this tale that we get our word *narcissist,* meaning "one who is in love with himself."

America has more than her fair share of narcissists; however, most of us who face "mirror-mirror-on-the-wall" each morning don't hear much about being the "fairest one of all." Not us. It's not that we have inferiority complexes; we *are* inferior. We may have our moments in the sun, where we shine brightly at something, but those moments don't last.

But accepting our inferiority is a hard sell. Instead, we try to overcome it with valiant effort and self-improvement gestures, evidences of a deep-seated fear in the soul—a kind of *inferiorphobia.*

NOT CREATED EQUAL

Not everything is the same. Differences abound. God intended it to be so. Apparently, He loves diversity. He didn't create just one kind of fern, but fourteen *thousand* different kinds. There is not just one type of flower. Every snowflake is different. Scientists estimate that there are at least a million different galaxies in just the section of sky framed by the cup of the Big Dipper. Diversity overkill. There are billions of humans—all unique. God loves that we are different, I think, and He wants us to act and look that way.

But with differences come judgments. People begin to say one thing is better than another, or one person is better than another—and in a way, they are right. It is difficult to accept that there are others superior to us. But, truth be told, there are. The idea that "all men are created equal" sounds great in the Declaration of Independence (and we should fight for it to be true politically), but it doesn't ring true in everyday life. We are *not* created equal. Some are smarter, faster, stronger, more beautiful to behold, and flat-out more talented. The same holds true for the rest of creation. But just because some are "superior" to us doesn't mean they are more significant. To think so is to think unbiblically.

The Bible claims that we matter—that we are God's dream come true. If we are *less*, then God made us so *with purpose*. The psalmist saw it. "I am fearfully and wonderfully made" (Ps. 139:14), he exclaimed. It takes great courage and grace to nakedly showcase and celebrate the differences that make us look *less*. But we need to be OK with naked—with letting our differences be seen.

They were "naked" is what the Bible says about the first people, Adam and Eve (Gen. 2:25). And they had no shame about it. It was only after they experienced the pain of sin that they resorted to sowing fig leaves together to cover their nakedness. The Scripture says they became "afraid" of their nakedness (Gen. 3:10). It's *what* they covered up that makes the story so compelling. They didn't cover their mouths, though their sin involved their mouths. They didn't cover their hands, though their hands were also involved. They covered the parts that were *different* from one sex to the other. Sin makes us afraid to display our differences—differences that some

21

judge as better or worse, superior or inferior. We all fear these judgments, so we hide.

But what if differences are good? What if God intended for there to be those who are more and those who are less, some who are flashy and some who aren't so arresting? Perhaps a big part of faith is resisting the judgments people assign to those differences, even when we land on the losing side of their judgments. But the idea that others are better than us elicits some pretty horrid feelings in our psyches—we are not *good enough*. We start asking ourselves the questions, *do I matter?* and *am I OK?* But the answers tend only to affirm our sense of insecurity and insignificance—and we rebel against them, because we all want to matter. On some level we all need to be needed. We need to be loved and appreciated. Nothing is more basic than that.

But what if worth isn't supposed to be determined by how we compare with others? What if we shouldn't be intimidated or feel put down because others outshine us in various ways? And who is to say that the judgments people attach to differences are accurate anyway?

I love the color red. But who is to say that red is better than green or blue or yellow, or all the shades in between? What if green felt bad about itself because it wasn't blue, or what if yellow cowered in shame because it wasn't red, or orange hid in fear because it wasn't a primary color? Don't all colors add to the whole of the experience of life?

I saw a huge painting recently of a rich chocolate liquid with what looked like the top of a dark red cherry swimming in it. The little dab of red set off the whole image for me. It was only a little part of the whole, but the contrast was stunning. What if the little dab of red tried to cover itself up because it wasn't the same as the prominent rich brown color that dominated the painting?

There is something in the human condition that wants to believe something is "best," which means, by comparison, that it is better than everything else. In this view, something or someone is at the top of the heap—"Best of Show." So, we are forever making comparisons and assigning judgments. Some things are judged wonderful; other things are judged worthless. There is no celebration of *all* differences and their intrinsic value, only juxtapositions in the quest of judgment.

THE PERFECT 10

There are examples all around us of people assigning unjustified values and rulings to differences. Take the issue of the "beautiful people," women in particular. Depending on where and when in human history, the value of a "10" was arbitrarily assigned to a particular look that was considered *beautiful*. Sometimes the 10s were tall; other times the short women won the day. There were seasons when fat women were favored and thin women shunned. Beauty has been assigned to large-nosed women, tiny-nosed women, tall-necked women, and stubby-necked women. I remember the first time I saw the bushy eyebrows of young Brooke Shields. Suddenly, someone decided to call that "beautiful."

Solomon had over a thousand wives. He spoke of a personal harem filled with "the delights of the heart of man" (Eccl. 2:8). He describes his *favorite* in the Song of Songs (7:4). This woman was the "10" of his day. He says her eyes were like "pools." Her nose was like the "tower of Lebanon" that overlooked Damascus (was it *long*?). Her neck was like an "ivory tower." Her breasts were like "two fawns" (Song 4:5). And get this: her belly was like a "mound of wheat" (Song 7:2). Not exactly Miss Universe by today's standards. But Solomon was howling.

Ever see the hotties from the Renaissance period? These were large, thunder-thighed women. I grew up in the fifties, and I remember that the babes of that day were also fairly curvaceous. So I will never forget the night that Twiggy the supermodel appeared on the popular TV show *Laugh-In*. Her name was completely appropriate. She was a virtual "twig," who was destined to become the new "10."

But the Twiggys who lived during the Renaissance went unnoticed. Many of the "thunder-thighed" women of today are ignored as well. The small-nosed women in Solomon's day weren't deemed gorgeous. But all varieties of appearance have been around since the dawn of time. Cultures simply assign some the role of beautiful and others the role of ugly. *But are any of these rulings valid?*

When women buy into these arbitrary values, the results can be devastating. They scramble to be who they aren't and often end up living superficial lives. The truth is, every woman is beautiful. At some particular time in history, every shape, size, and look was a 10—it just may not be the season for a specific kind of female to get the recognition that is due her.

Physical beauty is just one example of the dozens of ways comparisons are made between people in our world. It makes us wonder how valid other judgments about talent, money, intelligence, etc., really are. "Best of Show" based on comparisons changes from culture to culture and from generation to generation. In an agrarian African culture, the nomad sheepherder would have left Einstein looking like the village idiot. In the rock world, U2's Bono would have Luciano Pavarotti, the famous opera singer, booed off the stage. So here is the question: How can we gauge our personal significance by the comparisons and arbitrary judgments made by others? The apostle Paul wrote that those who "measure themselves by themselves and compare themselves with themselves" are "not wise" (2 Cor. 10:12).

As apprentices of Jesus Christ, we must consciously refuse to panic about differences. In fact, we should celebrate them. God designed us to be different. I'm not saying there is anything wrong with self-improvement or changing what we can about ourselves in response to the world in which we live. Those are good things. But the motive to do so should be to influence people for the cause of Christ, not to improve our own self-esteem. Paul writes, "I try to please everybody in every way. For I am not seeking my own good but the good of many, so that they may be saved" (1 Cor. 10:33).

But accepting and even celebrating differences is a strange concept to fallen human beings. Covering up differences is much more consistent with the trajectory of the Fall. When we honestly look at the differences between us and other people, we often feel that our significance is under attack. And we will continue to do so until we discover the way God views significance. He never intended for us to confuse *significance* with *prominence*.

PROMINENCE VERSUS SIGNIFICANCE

America is a hero culture. Prominence rules. Inconspicuous means insignificant. We search for people who stick out, who are worthy of adulation. We seek idols—American idols. We believe in being *stick-out* beautiful, *stick-out* rich, *stick-out* famous, and *stick-out* talented. *Stick-out* proves significance. If we don't *stick out*, if we are average or small in comparison to our heroes, we are losers. We certainly couldn't be small *and* be significant. Being big is what matters.

But does prominence *really* rule? One could argue that there are many *significant* things that are inconspicuous. Our eyes are obviously more prominent than our lungs, but are they more significant? We can live without eyes. My hands are more prominent than my liver, but I can't live without a liver. What if the small, hidden things are as significant as the big, prominent things? What if, at times, they are *more* significant?

In writing about the gifts and abilities of individuals in the church,

Paul says, "Those parts of the body that seem to be weaker are indispensable" (1 Cor. 12:22). "God," he writes, ". . . has given greater honor to the parts that lacked it" (v. 24). Think of that. God gives "greater honor" to those who are *less* prominent. God must see average Joes and Janes as the lungs and livers of the human race—maybe not prominent, but absolutely essential.

The biblical claim is that we were all calibrated by God to make us *fit* in this world where He wanted us to *fit.* Your personality (what makes you laugh, what makes you feel loved, how you make decisions, etc.) *was on purpose.* Your talents and abilities (or lack of them) all play into God's fitting you into specific places on earth for specific times to reach specific people. (See Acts 17:26.)

This is a cool idea *if* you happen to be as good-looking as Ben Affleck or Julia Roberts; or if you are as talented as Sting or Bono. But what if you aren't? What if you are kind of ugly, by media standards? What if you can't sing? What if you can't speak well in front of people or you aren't very smart? What if you have what some call a birth defect? What if your uniqueness is a *small* uniqueness—it only sticks out after people get to *know* you? Is it possible that God made you small *on purpose*?

The psalmist claimed that God created "small and great alike" (Ps. 115:13). What if God made you *small*? We are afraid of *small* in our culture. We think it means insignificant. But what if God doesn't agree? If you are an American who has been influenced by American culture, this thinking seems weird. After all, don't we all want to be in the spotlight? The popular reality-TV shows draw on making ordinary people famous. Isn't that what we should all want—to be BIG and famous?

But Jesus said, "What is highly valued among men is detestable in God's sight" (Luke 16:15). What if, in God's economy of thought, BIG isn't always best? What if *small* is often best? That would sure explain some things.

DARE TO THINK SMALL

Years ago, when my daughter, Elisabeth, was small, I was cleaning out a car I was trading in. When I checked under the driver's seat for any leftover treasure, I saw a cassette tape nestled about halfway back. The bucket seats were close to the floor, so my forearm was getting scraped up as I struggled to bag my prey, knees digging into the concrete. I succeeded only in pushing the cassette further beneath the seat with my fingertips. But I kept trying, reaching farther and farther, only to encounter the resistance of the fatter part of my forearm. My daughter saw me struggling and tried to get my attention.

"Daddy," she said, peeking over my shoulder into the car.

"Just a minute, honey," I responded.

"Daddy," she said a little more urgently.

"Hold on," I said insistently. "I'm trying to get this tape . . ."

"Daddy!"

I sat upright and snapped, "What do you want?"

She leaned past me, shot her little arm under the seat, and easily snagged what I was nearly committing suicide to get. As she handed me the tape and skipped off, I heard a gentle voice in my heart say, *Little fits where big doesn't.*

How do you feel when you run into someone who is bigger-than-life or stunningly talented? When I meet great people, most often I feel *less*. It's a bit like visiting the Grand Canyon. When you see amazing things, you tend to feel *unamazing*. God has chosen to make amazing people. But amazing people don't *fit* everywhere. They are too fat. That's why God makes all kinds of people. And one could argue that making people *less* talented and *less* gifted and *less* brilliant takes a lot of work.

My boys were young when Hasbro first came out with their Micro Machines. They were so cool. I couldn't get over the striking detail of those tiny cars and trucks. It is very difficult to create small

27

things with moving, functional parts. If you have been around the past thirty years, you have been stupefied at the progress made in the personal computing world. Engineers have tackled the seemingly impossible task of jamming more and more data and processing speed into tiny microchips. They have found a way to get the power of computers that used to fill whole rooms into chips that fit in your hand. But guess what? Those same engineers claim that creating the big stuff was much easier.

What if creating small people with small talent and ability is a greater miracle than making big, talented, brainy people? Could it have taken God more power to create something *less*? If you ask a professional singer to sing out of tune, it's tough. She alleges that it is harder for her to sing poorly than to sing perfectly. What if that is true with God?

Imagine standing on a beach and being hit by a seventy-foot tidal wave. The instant before the wave hits, you close your eyes, expecting to be swept away. Instead, as the monstrous wave passes, you are left standing on the shore with only one drop of moisture on your forehead. How could so much water leave so little of itself? What would you say? You would exclaim, "It's a miracle!" How does the only omnipotent Being in the universe, who is perfect and powerful and brilliant, creatively splash a person into existence who can't sing or dance or tackle math with ease? That had to be tough. Is small the greatest miracle of all?

THE POWER OF SMALL

As modern warfare developed, men tried to build bigger and bigger bombs. But some scientists began to suggest the greatest power was in the smallest place—the atom. And sure enough, when they figured out how to release the potential inherent in "small," it unleashed stag-

28

gering, never-before-seen power. The most force was in the smallest place. I wonder if the church of Jesus Christ loses ground because we keep looking for the next Billy Graham or Mother Teresa—for the big bombs. But what if the greatest power for God's kingdom is found in *small*, in the laity? Perhaps we should strive to release the potential inherent in at-home moms and dads, or in the butchers, bakers. and candlestick makers.

I love talking to people about God. I also love what happens in the preaching moment.

A few years back I was in Missouri, teaching at a men's retreat. Several hours before heading off to the retreat, I visited a mall. I was walking around, thinking and praying about the retreat, more than I was shopping, when I happened into a Successories store. As I started perusing the books and plaques, I noticed the salesperson out of the corner of my eye. She was facing the wall behind the cash register and talking on the phone. I immediately sensed something was wrong. I'm not much of a spooky, spiritual guy, but once in a while I feel a strong drawing of the Holy Spirit in everyday situations. This was one of them. I could see that she was crying. After she hung up the phone and tried to compose herself, I approached her.

"Excuse me, miss," I said softly. "I'm a pastor, and I was over there, looking at some of your stuff and minding my own business. But when I looked at you, I felt like God wanted me to come over here and pray for you. Is there anything wrong?"

Instantly she broke out in violent, gasping sobs, as tears squirted out of her eyes. Thankfully, no one else was in the store. She tried, but she couldn't talk, because of those little hiccupy sobs that little kids get.

"You don't have to say anything," I told her. "Is it OK if I pray for you?"

She nodded welcomingly.

"Jesus," I began, "I don't know what is going on here, but You do." I prayed for a few moments and then looked at her and asked, "Do you know anyone who is a person of faith, someone who believes the Bible?"

Again, she gave me a nod.

"Can you talk with him or her about what's going on?"

She agreed to do so. I prayed one more time for specific guidance and wisdom, then smiled and said good-bye.

As I left the store, I remember being surprised by how tangible the presence of the Holy Spirit was during the whole encounter. As I took a few steps into the mall, this thought hit me: *What if that was the most important thing you will ever do?* I was stunned at the thought. I immediately countered: *What about all the preaching? The writing? The counseling?*

My mind started to wander, and I began playing possible scenarios in my imagination. What if this girl was going to have an abortion, and this event halted that decision? And what if she has the baby; he grows up a believer, and he marries a wonderful Christian gal? Then *they* have a baby, who grows up and goes on a short-term missions trip to Argentina and wins a young boy to Christ, who later becomes a kind of Billy Graham to Argentina, winning millions of people to Jesus Christ?

And what if I am standing before God one day and He brings up the millions of people who came to Christ in Argentina, and says, "And you know who is responsible for these people's salvation?"

I see myself curiously wondering who.

"Ed Gungor!" God exclaims.

I'm flummoxed. "How can that be?" I ask.

"Do you remember that day in Successories? . . ." God says.

I'm not saying anything like that happened or will happen, but *what if* that is the way God does things? What if the ways God uses us are more covert than we could ever imagine? It's not that our preaching or writing or counseling isn't significant; it is. But what if the best is unleashed by things that seem small and irrelevant?

The Bible is chock-full of stories that exemplify this. A young woman named Ruth leaves her family and the land of her birth to care for the mother of her dead husband. Ruth is a Moabite woman; Naomi, her mother-in-law, is an Israelite. But Ruth's selfless dedication to Naomi is immovable. She tells her, "Where you go I will go, and where you stay I will stay. Your people will be my people and your God my God" (Ruth 1:16). When Ruth lands in Israel with Naomi, they are poverty-stricken. At Naomi's request, Ruth marries this guy who is twice her age, just to survive (the tone of the text suggests he was not an Abercrombie model). The story ends with Ruth giving birth to a son named Obed. Nice story, but that's about it.

Though the story of Ruth is sweet from one standpoint, it is so ordinary—so seemingly unimportant. But then we are surprised. Ruth, it turns out, is the great-grandmother of David, the greatest king in Israel's history, a man after God's own heart (Acts 13:22). The dedication and selfless love David shows in his life mirrors the same selfless commitments his great-grandmother Ruth had. I bet when Ruth met David in eternity and realized the connection, she was shocked. I'm sure she had no idea she was such a central player in God's kingdom enterprise. What if this is God's MO? What if God loves to weave the spectacular from the ordinary? And what if He loves to do it in a way that causes most to miss it—unless they are suspicious? What if being suspicious of God's activity is what faith is?

THE POWER OF SECRET

Some of the most significant things done by people are accomplished covertly. Many of our most powerful government agencies are covert, like the CIA, FBI, and NSA. And those who work undercover have power *precisely* because no one knows who they are. The agencies that break up crime find power in secrecy. Their agents don't have a public face. Their identities are hidden. It is to their advantage to come across as normal and unremarkable as they can. That's when they can best "fit in" and do their undercover work.

What if God has strategically placed believers all over the world in similar fashion? The Bible says, "The secret things belong to the LORD" (Deut. 29:29). What if we are being naive to think we are *only* maids or *only* taxi drivers, *only* waiters or mechanics? What if there are no *onlys* with God? What if we are *all* undercover for God as we take on the kingdom of darkness and call people "to open their eyes and turn them from darkness to light, and from the power of Satan to God" (Acts 26:18)?

Once, on CNN, there was a human-interest piece on a guy in Japan who had set up one million dominoes in a large field house. As thousands gathered to watch and the cameras were rolling, he knocked over the first domino, and the fun began. It took a long time for all the dominoes to tumble, one hitting the next. I remember thinking, *What if someone had snuck in and pulled a domino or two out of line?* How frustrating would that have been? But that is exactly what believers do to God all the time. Because we don't take ourselves seriously, because we don't think we matter, we step out of the game. We slack off and step back. I wonder how many times God is left grieving because we don't accurately evaluate who we are; we waste our lives, forcing God to come up with new strategies and new people to set in place for future gestures of redemption in the field house of life.

EMBRACING INFERIORITY

I saw a stage play once in which one of the minor actors had a hard time being a minor actor. He felt he should have had a larger role, so he ended up trying to expand his bit part into a bit *more*. He walked on and off the stage in an exaggerated way, and his lines were stretched and out of cadence with the other actors. Instead of lending what talent he had to the overall good of the show, his performance hurt it. Successful acting isn't about whether or not you are noticed or if you have the largest part, but by whether or not you play the role you are asked to play in a way that fulfills the writer's dream and the director's instructions.

Each of us is a destiny—a planned, on-purpose being that God wanted to cast in His unfolding play. If this is true, we can't think about life in terms of *making our own story*. Instead, we must each find our place in the story being told by God. This is a world where God has a purpose and a place for everything. Success and fulfillment should not be based on personal aggrandizement or actualization, but on obediently finding the position predestined for us by God.

In a world like this, small and great are irrelevant. They still exist. Some folks are amazingly bright and talented stars, while others of us are more like bit actors—but what difference does it make as long as both are *essential*? We may be different. But because we are God's creations, we cannot possibly be insignificant. Paul challenges us to embrace how we are made, saying, "But who are you, O man, to talk back to God? 'Shall what is formed say to him who formed it, "Why did you make me like this?"'" (Rom. 9:20).

We should embrace our inferiority, be OK with being less—even celebrate it. Who knows what God is up to? We might be changing the whole world. To fight inferiority feeds inferiorphobia, but we fight it because we believe inferiority is a sign that we are not significant. To *not* be significant makes it harder to breathe. We panic. We become like a drowning man—frantic and dangerous. So we pretend to be better than we really are. It is too painful to believe that we are worthless. But when we understand that inferiority is intentional, perhaps

33

even supermiraculous, and we understand it is the way God helps us "fit" in His master plan, we gladly embrace inferiority and find ourselves going undercover for God.

Sweet.

5

syncretitus: getting along with everybody

think everyone has to find his own spiritual path to God," my fellow shopper said.

I don't remember how we got on the subject of finding God. He may have asked me what I did for a living and I told him I was a pastor. However, we were in a deep conversation in the fairly long checkout line at Best Buy.

"Wouldn't that be cool if that were true?" I responded.

"What do you mean?" he queried.

"It would be cool if everyone *could* find his own spiritual path to God," I answered. "But that's not what Jesus said would happen. He said most people are missing the point and are on a road leading to destruction."

EVERYTHING IS RELATIVE

Unless you have been living in a bunker for the past thirty years, like Brendan Fraser in *Blast from the Past*, you know that we are living in a world of relativism. *Relativism* is the belief that all points of view are equally valid. What *you* think is right and wrong is right and wrong for you, and what *I* think is right and wrong is right and wrong for me. Though our lists may be completely different, each list is equally legitimate.

Relativism holds that what you believe about God and what I believe about God are equally good and equally true. There are no absolutes, no truth that is true for everyone, just relative ideas that are true to each one. Hence, what's good for me is not necessarily good for you, and vice versa. Everyone must find his or her own way.

But Scripture cuts right through the concept of relativism with the claim that God is the source of truth—not human reasoning or individual preference. This is a hard pill for moderns to accept. We are most likely to respond to the idea of absolute truth the way Pilate did. Jesus told Pilate, "I was born and entered the world so that I could witness to the truth. Everyone who cares for truth, who has any feeling for the truth, recognizes my voice."

Pilate responds, "What is truth?" (John 18:37–38 MSG).

Here is the challenge we face: How do those of us who buy into the idea of absolute truth fit in a world of relativism—a world that may be tolerant of our beliefs, but intolerant of our desire to export them? Jesus prayed concerning His disciples, "As you sent me into the world, I have sent them into the world." Jesus came to "witness to the truth." So must we.

DARE TO BE DIFFERENT

There are two basic truths we must hold as sacrosanct: first, human-kind is fallen, and second, we all need a Savior—we can't save ourselves. The Savior's name is Jesus. All other doctrines and practices in the church have some room for "relativity" in them. Of one such doctrine Paul wrote, "One man considers one day more sacred than another; another man considers every day alike. Each one should be fully convinced in his own mind" (Rom. 14:5). Some things are relative.

But refusing to move away from the basic truths of human depravity and the need for Jesus Christ poses huge problems. It means *everyone* must deal with the concept of sin and the person of Jesus Christ. Universal truths are untenable in a relativistic culture. As a result, Christians are often considered immaterial bigots in the public arena.

There are two ways we tend to respond to this (neither of which is appropriate). Either we get rigid and mean, which makes believers look exclusionary and gated, or we try to fit in by softening our commitment to the truth. We say (only if asked), "I follow Jesus, but everyone has to find his or her own way."

But holding hands with truth while trying to gain acceptance from those who don't is a form of *syncretism.* Syncretism is the fusing of different belief systems that don't naturally go together they may even be diametrically opposed to each other. And God doesn't think too highly of our attempts to do it. In the Old Testament, He brought judgment upon Israel over and over for it.

God wanted Israel to be *different*—to be "holy." But they wanted to fit in. "[We want to have what] the other nations have" was their constant cry (1 Sam. 8:5). But God had given Israel the laws they were to live by: from what to eat to what to wear to what to do on specific days. He did this for a reason; He told them, "Be holy, because I am holy" (Lev. 11:45). God is holy because He is *different.* So He gave Israel moral, ceremonial, and dietary laws to make them look unlike all the other nations of the world. He wanted them to be His, distinctively.

In the movie *Cleopatra,* there is a scene where the glamorous Cleopatra, with all her colorful clothing, beautiful hair and makeup, and opulent surroundings, is on her ship, cruising by a frumpy, homogeneous, meager-looking group of nomads. They were the Jews. The contrast between dazzling Egypt and this group was stark. God's *chosen* people didn't make being chosen seem all that enviable. But God didn't want them to "fit in."

How God loves, how He is motivated, and how He thinks is different from how any other being acts. God is unique. He says of Himself, "My thoughts are not your thoughts, neither are your ways my ways" (Isa. 55:8).

But He also says, "Learn from me" (Matt. 11:29). We who follow God need to understand that He is asking us to *represent* Him. Paul writes, "Don't become so well-adjusted to your culture that you fit into it without even thinking. Instead, fix your attention on God. You'll be changed from the inside out. Readily recognize what he wants from you, and quickly respond to it. Unlike the culture around you, always dragging you down" (Rom. 12:2 MSG).

We don't know what God was thinking when He created the stars or the plants or the animals, but we do know exactly what He was thinking when He created humans: "Let us make man in our image, in our likeness, and let them rule" (Gen. 1:26). God created us to look like Him and to expand His kingdom on the planet. Our purpose is to represent God and His rule in the world around us. How we make decisions, the kind of entertainment we participate in, the way we spend our money, our reactions to pressure and confrontation, our work ethic, how we manage our sexuality, how we treat others, all are to be representative of how God would do so, if He were human.

Being asked to be different in the world as His representative is a cool thing, but it is a *hard* "ask."

IT HURTS TO BE DIFFERENT

We don't want to be different. Being different draws rejection. And nobody likes rejection.

Some years back I read about a group of psychology students at the University of Berkeley who conducted an experiment. Without their chemistry professor's knowledge, they convinced the students of his class to listen intently, take careful notes, and look interested whenever the professor lectured near the radiator, which was by the window in the right front corner of the room. Whenever he moved away from it, they were to subtly begin acting bored and disinterested. By the end of the week, the professor was lecturing while *seated on the radiator!*

Whether we realize it or not, how people view us and treat us deeply affects us. C. S. Lewis said, "I believe that in all men's' lives at certain periods, and in many men's lives at all periods between infancy and extreme old age, one of the most dominant elements is the desire to be inside the local Ring and the terror of being left outside."[1] "To belong" is a siren song to the human heart—to not belong is pure torment. Yet being a follower of Jesus often guarantees rejection.

Jesus said, "If the world hates you, keep in mind that it hated me first" (John 15:18).

I was surprised when, after I gave my life to Jesus, I discovered not everyone shared my enthusiasm for Him. I wasn't prepared for the rejection I received, and it shook me at first. I almost stopped following the Lord. But being a fully devoted follower of Jesus means we must be willing to follow Him no matter who rejects us for it.

Jesus said, "The world would love you if you belonged to it; but you don't—for I chose you to come out of the world, and so it hates you." He went on to say that "since they persecuted me, naturally they will persecute you" (John 15:19–20 TLB).

Sometimes the persecution will come from people you love dearly, even those in your own home. That is really tough. But Jesus warned that faith sometimes causes a person's worst "enemies" to be "members of his own family" (Matt. 10:35–36 ICB). And He doesn't pull any punches. If we refuse to put Him above those we love, He tells us, "[You are] not worthy to be [mine]" (v. 37 ICB).

But what is it that makes people so mad at us? The first murder in history happened between two brothers, Cain and Abel. The Bible tells us that it occurred because Cain felt guilty and ashamed of his actions when presented with the right actions of his brother. Hatred dawned in Cain because Abel's good deeds made the evil deeds of Cain look *even more evil.*

"Do not be like Cain," John commands. He said Cain murdered his brother "because his own actions were evil and his brother's were righteous" (1 John 3:12). Then he warns, "Do not be surprised, my brothers, if the world hates you" (v. 13). That's the thing that makes people mad—when our actions appear "right," while theirs look wrong. No one wants to be wrong, especially in a world where nothing is wrong—everything is supposed to be *relative.*

CONEHEADS

Sadly, God's people have a history of trying to straddle the fence between the kingdom of God and the world around us—we long to fit in and belong. Though it was forbidden, the ancient Israelites even paid tribute to the pagan gods to open the door for trade and political power. They didn't want to stick with monotheism if it cost them jobs. Though God wanted to be their King, they begged him to give them a *real* king so that they could be like "all the other nations" (1 Sam. 8:5). God replied, "They have rejected me as their king" (v. 7). They were a little embarrassed about explaining to outsiders that their King was invisible. A visible king would help them seem more normal, like they were from this planet.

But God didn't want them to seem like they were from this planet; He wanted them to appear "as aliens and strangers in the world" (1 Peter 2:11) as "fellow citizens with God's people and members of God's household" (Eph. 2:19).

But historically God's people have acted more like Beldar and Prymatt from the *Coneheads* movie. This alien couple with cone-shaped heads came here from the planet Remulak to prepare for its invasion that was to take over the world. While waiting to be contacted by their mother planet, they adapt to earth customs, doing everything they can to fit in. But they enjoy life on Earth so much that they decide to abandon their mission to change the world, and a future life on Remulak. So they subvert the plan and make planet Earth their home.

Unwittingly, many believers are acting like Coneheads. We say we love the idea of heaven and that we are loyal to God; we say we want to help overcome the world by representing the kingdom of God, but secretly we have fallen in love with planet Earth, and we want to fit in. We act like, respond like, and seem like everyone else, often covering up our allegiance to Jesus or any attempts to be "more than conquerors" here (Rom. 8:37). If it is embarrassing or causes us to lose ground in some way, we don't even mention heaven.

We contract *syncretitus*. We spend tons of energy trying to reconcile godliness with worldliness—thoughts and beliefs that are diametrically opposed to each other. One cannot successfully mix faith with the unbiblical principles of the world in which we live. And if we try, we will lose our voice for God.

HOT OR COLD

"I know your deeds," Jesus tells a group of believers, "that you are neither cold nor hot. I wish you were either one or the other! So, because you are lukewarm—neither hot nor cold—I am about to spit you out of my mouth" (Rev. 3:15–16).

As a kid, I heard this text preached over and over again. Red-faced preachers would yell, "You can't be lukewarm! God wants you to either be on fire for Him, or to hate Him, but because you just sit there, you're going to get spit out—you're in danger of going to hell!"

That always made the crowd nervous and populated the altars. But something about it didn't sit right with me. Why would God rather have you "hate Him" than to be a bit casual about Him? And why would you merit hell for getting casual in your faith? Isn't going to heaven a free gift? Or is our message, "Accept Jesus, be red-hot for Him, and you'll get into heaven—but if you relax and get luke-warm, you better wake up quick and get red-hot again or you're going to hell"?

I don't think Jesus is talking about going to hell or about being fanatically "on fire" for Him versus hating Him. I think He is talking about the idea that if you want to be a "voice" for Him—to be in His mouth, you have to be willing to be different.

Think about it. If you take a cup of boiling water and a glass of freezing-cold water and leave them in a room for several hours, what happens? The boiling water cools, and the cold water warms—eventually they both become the *same* temperature as that of the room. Neither sticks out. Both fit in. They become lukewarm.

I think Jesus is crying out to these believers, saying, "Don't try to fit in the world around you! Don't long to be the same. I want you to be hot about some things and cold about others. If you say what everyone else is saying and believe what everyone else believes, you are the same as them. You can't stick out. You become the same temperature as those in the room with you—you are lukewarm. I won't be able to speak through you. I speak through *different*—hot or cold different. If you are unwilling to be different, you won't be able to represent Me—I will have to spit you out of My mouth."

No punishment of hell. No "God prefers me to hate Him." Just, no more syncretitus—we forego fitting in so we can speak for Him.

FRIENDS AND FAMILY

It takes a truckload of trust in God to obey Him even when family and friends reject you for it. But don't be afraid to let go of family and friends or jobs and circles of influence, if it takes that for you to stay true to your faith.

The good news is, God promises to make up for whatever we lose. Jesus said, "I tell you the truth. Everyone who has left his home, brothers, sisters, mother, father, children, or fields for me and for the Good News will get a hundred times more than he left. Here in this world he will have more homes, brothers, sisters, mothers, children, and fields. And with those things, he will also suffer for his belief. But in the age that is coming he will have life forever" (Mark 10:29–30 ICB).

There are three ways God rewards us for siding with Him: First, Jesus has followers everywhere, in every denomination. If you obey Him, He will lead you to them. You will be amazed at how the family of God is even more connected than families of origin, and much deeper than any natural friendships.

Second, over the years you will experience the joy of watching the very family and friends who initially rejected you come one by one into the kingdom of God! God will provoke them.

And third, there are eternal rewards when you stand for God while others reject you. Jesus said, "When others hate you and exclude you" because of your faith, you should "rejoice" and "leap for joy," because you "will have a great reward awaiting" in heaven (Luke 6:22–23 TLB). God will make the loss up to you forever.

Ever had a friend or relative stand up for you when others were against you? Feels pretty good, doesn't it? God loves it when people stand up for Him too, especially when it isn't cool or popular to do so: "Then those whose lives honored GOD got together and talked it over. GOD saw what they were doing and listened in. A book was opened in GOD's presence and minutes were taken of the meeting, with the names of the GOD-fearers written down, all the names of those who honored GOD's name" (Mal. 3:16 MSG). How priceless is that?

6

individualitus: just me and jesus

There is an old country song written by Tom Hall that goes:

Me and Jesus, got our own thing goin'.
Me and Jesus, got it all worked out.

Something about that sounds right. We Americans like being strong, individualistic, and tough. It's so . . . American. We are rugged individualists. And there is some good in that. But there is also danger.

Aristotle claimed that sharing our lives with one another is very important. He said that if "each man lives as he pleases," he lives "as the Cyclopes do."[1] The mythical Cyclopes were mean, destructive beings, with a single eye—for themselves. I think we evangelicals and charismatics stand guilty of that. Our lack of true community and intimacy and our rabid individuality have often made the typical American evangelical church monstrous.

We humans are by nature individual and communal beings. We were created that way. Throughout the first two chapters of Genesis, you find the phrase "and God saw that it was good" repeatedly. That was God's reply as He reflected on each aspect of the creation He had made. But after creating the first human, God said something very different. He looks at Adam and says, "This isn't good" (Gen.

45

2:18, author's paraphrase). He was referring to the fact that Adam was alone. God quickly moved to bring someone else into the picture. Community.

What's interesting in the narrative is that God essentially is saying human beings need more than just a relationship with God. We need other human beings! God designed us to need one another. Most think that needing or having to depend upon others is a sign of weakness. Our society teaches us that independence equals strength, when just the opposite is true.

It takes great strength to get along with others. We have to have a lot of intestinal fortitude and plain ol' guts to stay in relationships. All it takes is a well-developed attitude of selfishness to join the ranks of the Cyclopes. There is an abundance of that these days.

But God created us with a need for others. And that need was not the result of sin. Needing others is the plan and will of God. To feel actualized, we must find expression both individually and within the context of community. Sadly, in the evangelical/charismatic tradition there is little discussion about or awareness of the catholicity of faith.

James Sanders suggests that many in our culture "think of religion as a personal matter and concern, something between them as individuals and God."[2] Though few evangelicals would hold to the idea that community is inconsequential, our view of community is pretty pale. Perhaps our concept of individual faith has been so radicalized that we don't see the value of community.

But Jesus said one of the primary ways we show ourselves to be His disciples is by connecting with others who have faith (John 13:35). The idea is that faith is not to be lived out alone—*"just me and Jesus."*

What if grace, the power to change, is not just communicated to us when we are by ourselves? What if God designed faith to be more than just an intensely personal experience? It certainly is that, but what if God planned faith to have a corporate element as well? What if community—the idea of connecting with others—is a necessary conduit of critical grace in our lives? What if we are not just supposed to figure this out alone?

What if the deepest, deadliest, and most terrible parts of our lives never get uprooted until we can talk openly about them—confess them—to trustworthy others who can encourage us and lock arms with us to help us walk out our freedom?

This begs the question, do *you* have anyone like that in your life, someone with whom you can be totally honest? Or are you basically doing life alone? There are lots of us that are alone—and it can mean real trouble.

A NEW PARADIGM

I approach my whole ministry differently these days. I'm less interested in being leader-as-hero and I focus on trying to be a leader-as-fellow-journeyer. I'm less like the man behind the curtain in *The Wizard of Oz*—pulling levers and pushing buttons (putting on a great "head show")—and more like Dorothy, just the lead seeker running down the yellow brick road.

I'm also the quintessential bubble popper, because I tell people repeatedly that I don't have all the answers (and neither do the preachers who say they do). In addition, I like to boast about my weaknesses now, because I found out they have no power when they are in the light. I may not be perfect, but I do have a passion, like Dorothy, to find my way home—the place where God dwells—because "there's no place like home." (And I'm forever looking for more scarecrows, tin men, and lions to share the journey with me.)

I think we are in trouble as a culture, and I don't think the Church is doing much better. I think our greatest need is for community—for connecting with one another. Jesus never wrote a book, never established a school—His legacy was leaving a *community*.

The New Testament writings that we love and read devotionally, sprang from the living community Jesus left. We still have the writings. We still have His words, His truth, but I fear we have lost much of the idea of community—which is the Word (the writings) *incarnate*. (See 2 Corinthians 3:3.)

True, we have some huge churches with lots of numbers—the American church is big—but I am not sure we are all that significant, and I am quite sure there is little true connection. And I think people are starting to get tired of *big* and are longing more to *belong*.

So, what should we do?

REFUSE TO FLY SOLO

I think the biggest hindrance to community and belonging is that, for the most part, we do faith alone. We come to church and we hear thoughts about God, but then we are expected to figure out how to apply those thoughts on our own. It's as if the whole reason we come together is to hear the truth, and then we are to go off alone and try to figure out how to get it into practice.

Or we come together and we try to fix one another. Someone gets anointed and preaches and prays for people—maybe throws some oil on them or tries to expunge the devil—the goal is to *fix* people so they can, *again,* go off alone and successfully live out their faith.

Certainly, there is good in preaching and in praying and in ministering to one another. But what about the biblical imperative to "confess your sins to each other" (James 5:16)? Do *you* have someone in your life to whom you can *really* confess—with the confidence that he or she will not betray you, think less of you, or reject you? Will that person actually believe God is bigger than your weaknesses? Are you confident that, though this friend loves you, he will not accept your sin, but work with you to break through it?

48

How about the command that there should be "no division" in our midst and that every member in the church "should have equal concern for each other," so that when one member "suffers," every member "suffers with" him or her, and if one member is "honored," every member "rejoices with" that member (1 Cor. 12:25–26)? Is there anyone close enough to you who suffers when you suffer, or do you suffer in silence? Or is there anyone close enough to rejoice when you win at something? Someone you can tell when you're gaining ground, and who smiles with healthy pride and support of you?

THE DANGER

Certainly there are dangers associated with the idea of community. There are the obvious ones, like betrayal and legalism. Betrayal is easy to catch—it really hurts. And you can always smell legalism—you risk sharing a fault or a sin with a person, and you immediately lose stock value in his or her eyes—she treats you differently from then on. But the most dangerous aspect of connecting with others is our propensity to try to own other people's stuff—their problems.

If you are not careful, you will get sucked into the pain of the person you are trying to help instead of drawing him into the celebration and wholeness of your life. The Scriptures strongly warn to "watch yourself" whenever you get involved in helping others with their problems (Gal. 6:1). We are to help, but we must not make their troubles our own. Many individuals want you to do that, and it will burn you out. They are the "black hole" people. Black holes are those astronomical anomalies that scientists think are imploding stars that have such intense gravitational pull that not even light can sneak by without being sucked in. I know people like that. They are experts at drawing you into their dark, dark world. And before you know it, their darkness begins to become yours. In the words and waving arms of Robot from the ancient TV series *Lost in Space*, "Danger, Will Robinson."

Here is the key to staying safe: when you know *you* have spent a sufficient amount of time with the hurting person, you need to connect him or her with *other people*. You might say, "Why don't you get involved with that small group?" or "How about going and talking to so-and-so?" or "Let's get together with so-and-so and go over some of these issues together—they can get involved with us and help." If they are *not* "black hole" people, they will agree.

But here's what you'll hear from a dangerous person when you talk of getting others involved: "I don't really want to do that. I've talked to others. *You* are the only one who helps me. Can't *we* just talk?"

It's easy to overcommit to "black hole" people, because they know how to feed your ego—your need to be needed. It's wonderful to feel as though you are making a difference in the life of another. But *please* hear me. Run. Run for your life. Run while you *have* a life.

You may ask, "But what about the hurting person?" Don't worry. He or she will suck in another. These kinds of people don't miss a beat. They don't really want help anyway; they just want attention. Acting as if they need help appears to be the only way they know how to secure attention. This is a dark brood.

I HAVE A DREAM TOO

I have a dream of being part of a Christian community where you can be honest about your doubts and fears without being met with worn-out clichés or empty platitudes; a place that recognizes faith as a time-laded growth process, not the product of an "instant-pudding" altar prayer; a place where you can get help today but be challenged to grow so you're better prepared to face tomorrow; a place of intimacy, where you can know and be known; a place where it is hard *not* to find

God; a place where finding God is as corporate as it is personal; a place where you belong whether you're single, married, divorced, widowed, young, old, rich, poor, smart, dull, thin, fat, beautiful, or ugly; a place where you can find meaningful service, where you commit to something bigger than yourself; a place that *needs* you; a place of safety; a place off-limits to witches, demons, and the walking dead—the safest place in the world.

We could call it *church*.

pharisaic disorder: there is death in the pot

Pharisees suck eggs. That's the position Jesus took on them. At first blush His position is a little hard to understand. The Pharisees were the religious leaders of His day. You would think they would have been the good guys. They were the ones who kept all the rules—of course, they made up a bunch of them—so at least it *looked* as though they were trying to do what was right. But Jesus didn't see it that way. In fact, the Pharisees were the only group He openly campaigned against.

Jesus never came against the prostitutes, thieves, drunkards, or tax collectors (the closest thing to organized crime in Israel at the time) in His preaching. He befriended folks from those crowds. But He was completely at odds with the ministry of the Pharisees. Jesus consistently warned His followers to "beware of," to "be careful" about, and to "watch out" for the teachings and lifestyle of the Pharisees. They were the Eagle Scouts of religion. And their thinking was all out of whack.

It's difficult to catch the error of Pharisaic reasoning, because it begins with the Word of God—and we all are open to the Word of God. The problem wasn't in their desire to keep God's laws, but in the strategy they employed for keeping them. Jesus cautioned His followers about them: "Instead of giving you God's Law as food and drink by which you can banquet on God, they package it in bundles of rules, loading you down like pack animals" (Matt. 23:4 MSG). It was the "bundle of rules" they added to God's rules that made Pharisaic thinking dangerous. The additional rules became known as *fence laws*.

To ensure that a specific law of God was obeyed, the Pharisees believed they should make up rules that "fenced" people a step back from breaking the actual command. They thought of these "fence laws" as a first line of defense against disobedience. They reasoned that if a person would have to break the man-made fence laws before breaking one of God's real laws, it would be a deterrent and a protection for people. Noble enough.

But they ended up creating hundreds of fence laws dealing with everything from what one could wear or eat, to what one could or couldn't do on the Sabbath, and with whom. So, whether you wanted to pray, fast, rest, or *whatever,* there were dozens of rules to follow.

The problem was, there were too many of them to keep track of, much less follow. It wasn't possible to obey them all *unless* you devoted yourself completely to rehearsing and obeying them—which meant you had to *become* a Pharisee. There was no way the average illiterate Jewish person could keep up with these guys. So the masses of Israelites did the best they could, but pretty much resigned to the fact that they were lost. And the Pharisees gloated. They loved being the only really holy ones in Israel.

I know a few words in Spanish. I can say hello or ask where the bathroom is, but that's about it. If I would learn more words, I could communicate better with Spanish-speaking people. The Pharisees saw religious rules as a kind of God-language. And they were the only ones who spoke it! They believed the more rules a person knew, the more he or she would be able to commune with God. Their man-made rituals, formulas, and rules all brought people closer to God. But the truth was, what they added (which they believed helped them obey God) actually served to "nullify" the commands of God (Mark 7:13).

53

In a world of religious rule keeping, you have those who do and those who do not obey. The ones who do keep the rules always get the religious Eagle Scout badge, and they wear it with pride. Rule keeping puts you on the top perch, where you're forced to look down on others who are less than you—on all us messy spiritual Cub Scouts. And you can't help but feel a need to pressure those of us below you to obey the rules or else be disenfranchised—it's called "ministry." But it's really classic pharisaism.

BUILDING FENCES

Let's look at how fence laws are created.

Parents who love their children build similar kinds of "fence laws" all the time. Take the rule "Don't get hit by a car." Good rule. If you think about this rule long enough—and you believe you must do everything possible to ensure it will be obeyed—you might be tempted to bundle another rule to it, to add a "fence" that could serve as the first line of defense so that the actual rule you are ultimately trying to obey doesn't get violated.

One logical fence law to this would be "Don't play in the street." If you don't play in the street, a car won't hit you. That's reasonable.

But pharisaic thinking goes way beyond reasonableness and gets much more restrictive. Pharisaic thinking would go something like this: *The rule is, "Don't get hit by a car." We cannot allow anyone to be hit by a car . . . so, let's make sure that doesn't happen. Ah . . . let's make sure no one plays in the street—no street play will mean no one is hit by a car. Or better yet, it's probably best not to play outside at all, because then you won't happen into the street to get hit by a car.*

Or even better: Don't look out the windows of the house, lest you are tempted to think about going outside, which could lead into you wandering into the street to get hit by a car.

Or perhaps best of all: Play and sleep in the closet so you aren't tempted to look outside a window at all—because you know where that can lead . . .

The question becomes, at what point does the person we are trying to protect lose track of what the original law was all about? When she can't look out the window, or when she is kept in the closet? And that was the problem with the fence laws. They eventually overwhelmed the actual commands of God. Jesus said to the Pharisees, "You have a fine way of setting aside the commands of God in order to observe your own traditions!" (Mark 7:9).

But more than just distracting from God's law, these fence laws also became abusive. At what point does the legitimate desire to protect become a repressive system of abuse? Parents who make their kids live in closets need to go to jail. It doesn't matter if they started out loving, concerned, and protective. They end up controlling, manipulative, and repressive. That's Jesus' point about the Pharisees. The fence laws became weights that crippled faith, not helped it.

Are there modern-day Pharisees in the church? Yeah, kind of. I think there are many well-meaning Christians (laypeople *and* leaders) who, though they are not whole-hog Pharisees, think a lot like the Pharisees of old. That should cause us great concern. I don't think Christians get weak and tired in their faith because of a lack of Bible study, accountability, prayer, small groups, or church attendance. I think we tire because of the boatloads of pharisaic, legalistic thinking we have thrown at us.

MODERN FENCE LAWS

Sadly, modern fence laws abound in the church. For example, the Bible commands us not to get drunk with wine. A simple, clear command. But instead of preaching about drinking in moderation (which is considered too dangerous and way too messy), many groups add

the fence law of never drinking a drop of alcohol at all—total abstinence. This is so pervasive in American churches that most evangelical and charismatic churches use grape juice for holy Communion.
We can't talk truthfully about the bread and the *wine*; it's the bread
and the "juice." There is nothing wrong with this choice, but it is a
human fence law, not God's. But for a number of groups, the total
abstinence fence isn't enough. Not nearly.

To ensure complete holiness, some groups add additional fence
laws like: "Don't even go into restaurants that serve alcohol." Or some
modify this law: "You can go to a restaurant that serves liquor, as long
as they don't have an open bar." I know of churches that chastise
members if they are seen eating at a restaurant that sports an open
bar. The "do-not-get-drunk" command of God is eclipsed by the
"don't-eat-at-*that*-restaurant" rule. And we cannot intelligently answer
our kids when they ask, "Why can't we eat at that cool restaurant?"

I believe people with good intentions make these kinds of rules.
But the more our faith becomes about keeping human rules, the
more lifeless it becomes. That's the position Jesus took on this. Faith
can easily stop being about God and His guidance in our lives and
start being more about the opinions of others and how they think we
should live. It can quickly become a dead, human, religious thing.

MORE FENCE LAWS

The Bible clearly warns us against "worldliness," which is a love for
this world and its accoutrements, more than a love for God and His
kingdom.

I met Pastor Joe while I was still in high school back in the early
'70s. I had given my life to Christ about two years before but still
wore the clothes and hairstyle that were popular for my generation.
And Pastor Joe was concerned. He felt that my clothing was

"worldly." Pastor Joe was an old-school conservative, who felt that worldliness could be best avoided by a couple of fence laws that would preempt one from going down the worldliness path.

"I'm concerned about you, Ed," he told me as he pulled me aside one day. "I feel like you are still carrying the marks of worldliness. The Scriptures tell us to 'love not the world, neither the things that are in the world'" (1 John 2:15 KJV). He continued, quoting exclusively from the King James text. "And I fear you are in love with the world."

"Why do you think that?" I asked, confused because I had really sold out for God in my heart.

"Why, look at how you are dressed—and your hair," he answered. "You look like a hippie. You are communicating rebellion, sexual promiscuity, and drug usage everywhere you go."

The truth is, clothing and hairstyles do not necessarily reflect what is going on in the heart. I was certainly not dressing lewdly (remember the baggy-legged, disheveled hippie look of the '70s?), and though I looked like what was associated with drug addiction and youthful rebellion in Pastor Joe's mind, I was just dressing the way kids my age dressed.

He went on to ask me, "Don't you admit that what we wear speaks to people?"

"I guess," I replied.

"Well, what do you think your clothing is speaking, versus what I am wearing?" he asked.

"I think my clothing is saying, 'I like to be comfortable,'" I told him. But he wasn't buying it. He told me I needed to wear what he was wearing.

Pastor Joe always wore dark pants; black shoes; a pressed, white shirt; and a plain, dark tie. He would have looked like a stand-in for *The Blues Brothers*, but he had a 1961 haircut, so he wasn't nearly as cool.

I told him I couldn't imagine wearing what he had on. Then I said, as kindly as I could, that I thought the way he dressed was "speaking" that he was an extra from *Leave It to Beaver*. I added that if I tried to dress like him, my friends would think I thought it was Halloween. The conversation went south from there.

It's been thirty-five years since that conversation, and I still run into people who feel like Pastor Joe. They feel that being fashionable is worldliness. I guess they reason that if they are "fashionless," they will never get anywhere near becoming worldly. Hence, if you want to see what was in style a few years ago, just watch Christian TV or visit a few evangelical or charismatic churches this Sunday. These groups often contend by example that being out of sync with style is a mark of holiness.

But God says nothing about style in the Bible. He does warn us about loving this world too much. But does that translate into wearing clothing that is eight to ten years out of style?

PROMISCUITY FENCE LAWS

The Bible has clear prohibitions against dressing inappropriately or provocatively (1 Tim. 2:9). The Bible is certainly not propornography. Physical privacy is the standard. But a number of fence laws surrounding this legitimate command of God actually border on insanity.

Before addressing this, I need to say that I have worked with Christian day schools for many years and am very aware of the sacrifice and devotion many in Christian education make. They are wonderful people. But sometimes wonderful people can do pretty wacky things.

At one Christian school I know of, someone determined that the Abercrombie label was inappropriate for Christians to wear because of the soft-porn look of their catalog. I had never seen an Abercrombie catalog, so I wasn't offended when I heard about it (though I thought the proper response would have been to encourage folks who get their buttons pushed while looking at the catalog, to not look at it).

I remember my friends and I being lured into the women's section of the Sears catalog as teenage boys, the pages where the models are scantily clothed. We soon decided as followers of Jesus that we needed to find ways to connect with the grace that helped us say no to the things that sent us down wrong paths. But we never thought of boycotting Sears wear; we just left the catalog alone.

In response to the Abercrombie catalog, the school decided to add a new fence law—presumably one that would protect the children from becoming porn addicts. The law was, no child enrolled could sport Abercrombie clothing. Never mind that the only clothing allowed was a uniform consisting of khakis, a tucked-in polo shirt, a belt, and dress shoes. And never mind that Abercrombie khakis, polos, and belts weren't any more "pornographic" than any of the other brands. The law had been made: *No Abercrombie.*

Because it was so difficult to tell the Abercrombie clothing from other labels, the administration decided they needed to check the labels on the children's clothing to ensure Abercrombie wasn't being sneaked in. One teenage parishioner shuddered as she told me she was required to *bend over* in front of a male teacher, who pulled down the back of her pants to check the waistline's label. All for holiness, of course.

The parents' response was a decision that she'd fare better in a different school.

While recalling this story, I couldn't help but remember the words of Jesus:

> "You're hopeless, you religion scholars and Pharisees! Frauds! You keep meticulous account books, tithing on every nickel and dime you get, but on the meat of God's Law, things like fairness and compassion and commitment—the absolute basics!—you carelessly take it or leave it. Careful bookkeeping is commendable, but the basics are required. Do you have any idea how silly you look, writing a life

59

story that's wrong from start to finish, nitpicking over commas and semicolons?" (Matt. 23:23–24 MSG)

I recently heard of a new fence law against thongs—as in women's underwear. There are actually churches preaching this prohibition from the pulpit! I couldn't help but wonder how they are going to police this to ensure the disciples embrace this level of holiness? The Pharisees of Jesus' day went into the cupboards in people's homes to see if they tithed from their spices. Perhaps this group will do home checks on this issue . . .

It is precisely this kind of silliness that caused the stern reaction of Jesus against the teaching of the Pharisees. Faith is not about this kind of thing.

Do people actually love God *more* when they are strapped to fences like this? Not at all. This stuff gets church people tired and cranky while serving no spiritual purpose whatsoever. This is an example of pharisaic legalism. The fence laws make you forget God's original command altogether. Faith becomes all about rule keeping and judgment throwing. Welcome to Phariseeville.

But please hear me. It is not evil people who make up these rules. I think they are honestly attempting to protect people (unlike the Pharisees of old). Very few in the church qualify as full-fledged Pharisees. But Jesus' warning to His disciples about the infectious way Pharisees think is still valid for us. "Be careful," Jesus said to them. "Be on your guard against the yeast of the Pharisees" (Matt. 16:6).

BAD CUCUMBERS

"There is death in the pot!" was the cry of a bunch of prophets-in-training under a very powerful Old Testament prophet named Elisha (2 Kings 4:40). Apparently, someone had innocently thrown some poisonous "squirting" cucumbers, indigenous to that region, into a stew. I suggest that this is precisely what has happened in the modern-day stew we call Christianity. There is death in the pot. The bad cucumbers are the poisonous rules and ways of the Pharisees—their teachings.

This is why there are so many Christians who are weak and tired and burned out—too many "bad" cucumbers in their diet. This is why many of our teens are exiting churches. Jesus is cool. He isn't the problem. We are. We force our kids to grow up playing in the closet because we are afraid of them ending up in the street. We think it's too risky to invite them to consider the reasonableness of God's commands; instead we treat them like pack animals who must carry our *musts* and *shoulds* and *you-betters* from our never-ending garden of squirting cucumbers.

THE CURE

The cure for pharisaic thinking is simple: we must trust God's own work in people and let the truth of God's Word stand on its own. But we are afraid of that. I think Adam was afraid of that in the Garden of Eden. And he did with Eve what the Pharisees did and what we do over and over—Adam created fence laws for Eve.

God had said to Adam, "You must not eat from the tree of the knowledge of good and evil, for when you eat of it you will surely die" (Gen. 2:17).

But Adam adds a nice fence law to this and communicates to Eve, "You must not eat fruit from the tree that is in the middle of the garden, *and you must not touch it*, or you will die" (Gen. 3:3, emphasis added).

God never said anything about touching it. They could have juggled it, played catch with it, played "fruitball" with it—they just weren't supposed to *eat* it. But I can just hear Adam saying, "Eve, see this fruit?

61

Don't eat it. We're not supposed to eat it." Then, in order to protect her, he adds, "In fact, just *don't even touch it* or we are going to die."

God was willing to trust Adam's reasonableness, but Adam wasn't going to go there with Eve. No way. After all, if she thought about it, she might be OK with touching the fruit—that would be one step closer to trouble. Fruit fondling may have been too close for comfort from Adam's perspective, so why not be safe and eliminate *all* contact? A little loss of freedom in the name of safety is a good thing. Right? But that is the root of all pharisaic thought. And it's a bad cucumber.

Leaders (including parents) do this all the time. We don't just give people the truth and trust God to help them contextualize it in their unique set of circumstances with their unique personalities; we interpret and make deductions about the truth *for* them. We just feel it's safer.

We don't tell believers to avoid drunkenness as the Scriptures teach; we tell them to never drink at all. It's just safer. We don't say to simply avoid lewd actions that tempt the opposite sex, as the Scriptures teach; we forbid them to *ever* dance or wear short skirts or tight pants, or even touch one another.

Our intentions may be good, but adding to the commands of God is never smart. Jesus warned the Pharisees about adding their presumptions and interpretations to the Word of God: "You nullify the word of God by your tradition that you have handed down. And you do many things like that" (Mark 7:13). When we *add to* the truth or teach our application of the truth instead of the naked truth, we actually nullify the Word of God and make faith about human tradition. We add "death" to the pot of faith.

There is something of wonder in the fact that God trusts us, that He believes in us, that He allows us to process life with Him. It would be easier, it seems to me, to enforce repressive and prohibitive rules rather than allowing this kind of freedom. But what if it's a freedom that leads to life?

8

affluenza: i want more

Success is good; affluence is good. But does that mean God guarantees everyone on the planet a place among the rich and famous? The Bible tells us that money is both wonderful and deadly. These two divergent streams are strongly articulated throughout the Bible, which creates some perplexity. A lot like life, I guess.

It is clear that God does bless humankind with physical goods. However, equivocating success with godliness is a scriptural no-no. Jesus said the kingdom of God belongs to poor people (Matt. 5:3). Some individuals in Scripture "joyfully accepted the confiscation" of their property, because they were godly (Heb. 10:34). In other words, they were poor—*poor and godly*. Others, called heroes of faith, "went about in sheepskins and goatskins." They were "destitute" and "mistreated" (Heb. 11:37). They didn't have nice homes: "They wandered in deserts and mountains, and in caves and holes in the ground." And the Bible says these folks were so holy that "the world was not worthy of them" (v. 38). Wealth is not a symbol of spirituality.

But before we go there, let's talk about the wonderful side of money. We'll see that money *is* a blessing from God and, perhaps more surprising, it can actually enhance our relationships with God.

THE WONDERFUL SIDE OF MONEY

You don't have to go very deep into Scripture to discover that God loves to lavishly provide for His creation. The Garden of Eden was a place of abundance. There was a plenitude of food and other natural resources, and it was said, "The gold of that land is good" (Gen. 2:11). And consider the description given at the end of the Bible of the main street of our eternal home: "The great street of the city was of pure gold, like transparent glass" (Rev. 21:21).

God loves gold. He loves nice things. He was the one who made the physical world with all its wealth and called it all "good" (Gen. 1:31).

Some take offense when people talk about trusting God for financial and material needs. They think it's being selfish. They assume we don't have the right to pray about anything but spiritual things and that, since God knows what we need before we ask Him (Matt. 6:8), we should leave the whole enterprise in God's hands.

But God wants us to trust Him in every part of our lives, not just the spiritual parts. When you watch and listen to Jesus, it is obvious that earth is God's province and He loves to jump into our earthly stuff. Catherine Marshall writes:

> If we are to believe Jesus, his Father and our Father is the God of all life and his caring and provision include a sheepherder's lost lamb, a falling sparrow, a sick child, the hunger pangs of a crowd of four thousand, the need for wine at a wedding feast, and the plight of professional fishermen who toiled all night and caught nothing. These vignettes, scattered through the Gospels are like little patches of gold dust, say to us, "No creaturely need is outside the scope or range of prayer."[1]

In other words, _God cares about what we care about._
Back in the day when I first came to Jesus, every serious believer

I knew talked only about surrender, sacrifice, and giving up our lives for the cause of Christ—the deeper life. We used to sit around and muse about how cool it would be to actually die for our faith. We never thought much about praying for God to provide for us. We thought faith was about surrendering control to Jesus Christ—if He provides, great; if not, we die smiling. We were a die-to-self, suffering kind of crowd. But there were problems.

Hard became a badge of spirituality for my buds and me. And we all walked around looking as though we were baptized in lemon juice. We were big on the deeper life, but things got so deep that it was getting harder and harder to breathe.

When Gail and I first heard that God wanted to answer specific prayers about material things, it was a bit of a stretch for us. It seemed so selfish and wrong. Worldly. But the promises were everywhere in the Bible. Verses like "And my God will meet all your needs according to his glorious riches in Christ Jesus" (Phil. 4:19). And though I tried to spiritualize this to mean "spiritual needs," the context is obviously financial. After some study it became clear to me: God cares about money *and* physical provision.

Our first "provision" miracle happened with a rental property. After Gail and I married in 1976, we lived in an apartment we mockingly called "the Palace." It had slanted walls, one space heater (we lived in frigid Wisconsin), and a toilet and tiny shower in the closet. We were paying $90 a month.

Some friends of ours in St. Louis told us how they got a home for $240 a month in a market where similar homes were going for close to $500. They said they looked at their budget and asked God for a home in that price range. Gail and I thought that if God did it for our friends, He would probably do it for us.

We examined our budget and decided that, though it would be a stretch, we could probably afford $125 a month. We prayed, "Lord, we wouldn't even ask about this if we hadn't run into Bible promises that say You care about these things. We ask You to give us a home for $125 a month. We trust You to do it." Then we watched the paper.

We had already been perusing the paper for about a month, but there were no rental homes for less than $300. But three days after we prayed, an ad appeared for a two-bedroom home—for *$125* a month. We went to see it, did a Jericho march around it (if you don't know what that is, that's probably a good thing), and thanked God that it was ours.

When we called, an elderly lady answered and said, "I'm probably asking too little for the house. I have had so many calls about it."

We went to meet with her, and as we were talking, a professor from the local junior college called and offered her more money for the property. Gail and I just bowed our heads and said, "We thank You, Father, for our $125 house." We knew it might not be *this one*, but we suspected that it would.

"Thank you for the offer," she said on the phone, "but I want to give it to this nice young couple."

It's hard to describe the potpourri of feelings we had. We were elated. It humbled us. We felt loved and cared for. We felt undone, broken by the fact that almighty God cared about something so domestic, so common. This wasn't a missionary house or a home for wayward teens—it was where Ed and Gail Gungor lived. And God moved to make it so. We knew this answered prayer wasn't proof of our spirituality or a badge of maturity; it was a simple God-story. And we felt kissed—it was our *first* "provision kiss" from God.

When you see God provide for you, it impacts you spiritually. The Bible says one spiritual result of God's supernatural provision is *joy* (Deut. 16:15). But there is more. You feel His love and embrace. It breeds hope for the future. God's provision fosters wonder and awe—this is the *wonder*ful side of money. Jesus said if we know how to give good gifts to our children, how much more will our Father in heaven give good gifts to those who ask Him (Matt. 7:11)! It is just *too* sweet to discover He really is *our* Father.

Many of the rich folks whose stories are sprinkled throughout the Bible, credited God for their wealth. Once Abraham told someone who tried to give him a reward, "I will accept nothing belonging to you, not even a thread or the thong of a sandal, so that you will never be able to say, 'I made Abram rich'" (Gen. 14:23). He knew his wealth was the result of *God's* blessing.

God once said to Solomon, the richest king in Israel's history, "Since you have asked for [wisdom] and not for long life or wealth . . . I will give you what you have not asked for—both riches and honor—so that in your lifetime you will have no equal among kings" (1 Kings 3:11–13). This guy used to stack silver in the streets, because it was basically worthless compared to the amount of gold in his possession. When buying from other nations, Israel used silver but demanded gold for its own sales. Later, Jesus used Solomon as the model when He talked about the Father providing for the needs of His followers (Matt. 6:29).

We could mention Job—the Bill Gates of his day; the rich women who supported Jesus' ministry (Luke 8:2–3); wealthy Joseph of Arimathea, who offered his first-class tomb for the Lord (John 19:38); and the list goes on and on.

The possibility of joy, worship, obedience, adventure, and influence are all wrapped around the wonder of money. Bible guys like Zacchaeus experienced conversion when he offered a bunch of his money (Luke 19:8); the rich young ruler had a shot at that, but turned it down (Mark 10:21); and Jesus said our hearts could be kept clean if we deal rightly with money (Matt. 6:21). But these adventures of wonder are only possible when we possess money without being possessed *by* money. It's being possessed *by* money that turns this subject dark.

THE DARK SIDE OF MONEY

Money can be deadly. And the warnings given about money in the Bible are severe. Jesus said, "Woe to you who are rich" (Luke 6:24). He warned, "Watch out! Be on your guard against all kinds of greed; a man's life does not consist in the abundance of his possessions" (Luke 12:15). In some cases, Jesus went so far as to command, "Sell your possessions and give to the poor."

What do you do with texts like these?

First, we simply listen. No rationale. No explanations. Just listen. Something begins to emerge when we get still and let these texts speak for themselves. It's a little terrifying to listen, but we all need a good scare now and again—especially in this business of money.

One thing pops up loud and clear: *money can be a threat to our faith.* It is a threat because it is not just a neutral thing that we possess, like a car or a pet; it is a kind of alternative god that vies for our adoration. Jesus claimed, "No servant can serve two masters. Either he will hate the one and love the other, or he will be devoted to the one and despise the other. You cannot serve both God and Money" (Luke 16:13).

There is something about money that competes for people's devotion. People serve money the way they serve God. Why? Because money transfers to its owner certain godlike features. For example, God is omnipotent (all-powerful), but those who possess lots of cash *feel* omnipotent, as though they can do anything they want. God is omnipresent, but wealth also carries a hint of omnipresence, because the wealthy believe they can go anywhere, anytime. God alone is omniscient (all-knowing), but the rich come to believe they can find out whatever they want—again, a rumor of the Divine.

We cannot be casual about this. The first commandment of the Decalogue is "You shall have no other gods before me" (Ex. 20:3). And money is a rival god. Paul warned that "the love of money is a root of all kinds of evil" and that "some people, eager for money, have wandered from the faith and pierced themselves with many griefs" (1 Tim. 6:10).

Most preachers who overemphasize prosperity are completely silent about money's dark side. It's as if they believe money is *only* good, and the more we get, the better. They even go so far as to say that prosperity is a sign of spiritual health and strong faith. Crudely stated, the message is "If you love Jesus, you'll get rich."

But Jesus never bought into the idea that affluence was a sign of spirituality. In fact, He tended to espouse quite the opposite. He said it would be "easier for a camel to go through the eye of a needle than for a rich man to enter the kingdom of God" (Matt. 19:24). No spiritual warm fuzzies there.

Paul warned about "false" church leaders who asserted "that godliness is a means to financial gain." He said those teachers were "conceited," "unhealthy," and had a "corrupt mind" (1 Tim. 6:3–5).

Just flip on the TV and you will find preachers who, while ignoring the texts that warn about prosperity's deadly aspects, promise viewers that godliness and wealth go hand in hand. They brush off the idea that money is a kind of force that competes for the affection of the human heart, as Jesus warned. They completely disregard the biblical warning that no "greedy" person has "any inheritance in the kingdom of Christ and of God" (Eph. 5:5). And they neglect to point out that the greedy are inviting "God's wrath" into their lives (v. 6). Instead, they just tell people to trust God for *more*. And if we send money to *their* ministries, we are promised more will come. We all need more, right? And then we need more to *take care of* our more. Eventually it becomes hard to focus on anything else, and we contract "affluenza."

FREEDOM FOR WEALTH

The secret to experiencing the wonderful side of money, where you enjoy the provision of a loving Father, God, while staying free from money's dark, idolatrous pull, is the act of *giving*.

Giving touches a nerve in us that nothing else does. We look a lot like God when we do it: "For God so loved the world that he gave . . ." (John 3:16). When you give, you defy the fear that you won't have enough. You insult greed, the impulse to acquire or possess more than one needs or deserves. You frustrate avarice, the insatiable desire for wealth, and one of the historical seven deadly sins.

Money becomes soul destroying when we use it to taste omnipotence, omnipresence, or omniscience—when we seek power and position. It ravages the heart when we allow a longing for money to bind us with fear and greed. All this is obviated and kept at bay in the act of giving.

If you really believe God owns it all and that He is your source and provider, giving will be a simple matter. Contrariwise, if you believe that what you have is *yours* and you're unsure whether God had anything to do with getting it to you, you will hold on to your money for dear life. The arena of giving is the *only* place where exactly what's going on in your heart is revealed. That's why Jesus talked so openly about money and giving. In fact, He spoke more on this subject than any other, except the kingdom of God.

According to Jesus, giving keeps your heart in motion toward God and away from material things. That's what He was talking about when He said in the context of giving, "Where your treasure is, there your heart will be also." Your heart will follow the direction of your giving. If we throw money at (give to) things that bring glory to God, our hearts will be running toward God.

Here are some things we can do to cultivate a lifestyle of giving, which will keep us free enough to enjoy the wealth God brings:

Practice contentment. Paul said he has learned a great secret of life: "I've learned by now to be quite content whatever my circumstances. I'm just as happy with little as with much, with much as with little. I've found the recipe for being happy whether full or hungry, hands full or hands empty. Whatever I have, wherever I am, I can make it through anything in the One who makes me who I am" (Phil. 4:11–13 MSG).

Unless we are content with what we have, we have no grounds for asking for more. That would be evidence of greed, lust, or an inordinate love for this world. The psalmist warned about "men of this world whose reward is in this life" (Ps. 17:14). This is not our world. We are "aliens and strangers in the world" (1 Peter 2:11), citizens of another place (Phil. 3:20).

Commit to spending less than you make so resources are available for others. Don't spend all you have on yourself. Leave some for others. Let your spending habits be tempered by *their* needs, both spiritual and material.

Gratefully acknowledge God as your source. Paul wrote, "What do you have that you did not receive? And if you did receive it, why do you boast as though you did not?" (1 Cor. 4:7). We need to practice acknowledging God as the source of all the wealth we have. The Bible says it is God "who gives you the ability to produce wealth" (Deut. 8:18). This will help us hold things loosely—we own things without treasuring them and possess things without becoming possessed by them.

Trust God for increase so you can give joyfully and generously. Jabez prayed to God, "Oh, that you would bless me and enlarge my territory!" (1 Chron. 4:10). There is nothing wrong with praying for increase and for success—unless there are hidden reefs of discontentment, greed, idolatry, and lust in your heart. James warned, "When you ask, you do not receive, because you ask with wrong motives, that you may spend what you get on your pleasures" (James 4:3). The actual practice of giving will keep your heart clean and position you to trust God for material increase.

But giving doesn't mean not enjoying what we have been given.

For centuries many saints have believed that poverty was a sign of spirituality. But that is as much an error as believing prosperity is a sign of spirituality. Remember, for every mile on the road of truth, there are two miles of ditches.

THE GRACE OF GIVING

Paul calls giving a *grace* (2 Cor. 8:7). It's a *grace* because it is based on love. The giving gesture was modeled by Jesus when "though he was rich . . . for your sakes he became poor" and His motive was so *others* would "become rich" (v. 9). This should be the true motive behind giving: love for others. Not *give-so-you-can-get*. And that is my problem with many of my preaching colleagues. They are unwary when they approach this, and, intentionally or unintentionally, they end up teaching that we are to give *so we can get*. I understand there is truth to the law of sowing and reaping and that giving *does* open the way for us to receive more from God, but I believe this has been radicalized in many circles to the point that it is more false than true. And I believe it has become a cover-up for materialism.

Week after week, on television and in many churches, ministers come up with dozens of schemes to get people to give more money. Most of these are "give-to-get" schemes, everything from "pledges" to "hundredfold-return" offerings to "get-this-special-prayer-cloth-for-your-gift-of $___ offerings," and the saints of God are milked for dollars. These ministers continually ask people to "partner" with them, yet interestingly, Paul said of those whose thinking about money is skewed, "Therefore do not be partners with them" (Eph. 5:7).

A good friend of mine is a traveling minister. Once, he was speaking at a fairly large charismatic church known for its missions and outreach. It is not uncommon for two or three offerings to be taken in each of their weekend services. The pastor approached my friend before the service and asked him if he wanted to receive his own offering. My friend said he was open to whatever the pastor wanted.

Then the pastor asked him, "Don't you have some special project going on? People like to give to projects. If you give them one, they'll give more."

My friend was horrified.

I'm sure the pastor was trying to be helpful, but does anyone else think that is just a little weird? OK, I'll say it. It's weird. *The emperor has no clothes.*

And while I'm at it, it's probably just a coincidence that the key to wealth promised by the prosperity preachers is always the giving of "love gifts" and "pledges" to *that* particular televangelist or church organization. One has to wonder . . . if what they say is *really* true, why don't they just tell people to give, period—to whomever. And why don't these preachers just do the same, instead of asking for money?

Think about it for a minute. If everyone does get a hundredfold return from giving, why not just grab a hundred dollars and give it? That would yield ten thousand more. Give that ten thousand dollars and it would yield a million more. Then, if they give the one million—that would yield one hundred million! Just a few "givings" and their whole television or church ministry would never need another outside dime.

If the whole church would get in on this, in a short while we would have all the money in the world, and then we could start trusting God to get it from one another. One day there would only be one with it all, and if I have enough faith, it will be me . . .

9

sovereignty shingles:
God and the five-hundred-pound gorilla

I met Bruce in St. Louis, Missouri, in the early 1970s. He had a wry smile and squinty, Santa Claus eyes that were full of life. When I first spoke with him, I thought he was a new believer. He had way too much joy to have entered the "deeper life" with all of us "mature" believers.

"So," I asked him, "how long have you known Jesus?"

"About six years," he replied.

Six years! I thought to myself. *That's two years longer than I have been a believer! How can he be so happy?*

"Wow, six years!" I blurted out. (That's a near eternity in teen years).

"Yep," he replied, smiling ear to ear, "It's wonderful following Jesus, isn't it?"

"Yeah," I said, sounding a little less convinced than he sounded.

Bruce shook me up that day. I didn't get how he could be so happy after being a believer for longer than *six months*, much less six years. I decided he must be faking a little, so I asked him for his phone number and told him I wanted to talk with him some more.

Over the next eight months or so, I called Bruce repeatedly. He didn't know it, but my hope was that I would catch him having a bad day.

"Hey, Bruce, how are you doing?" I'd always ask, crossed fingered and hoping I would find him down and discouraged, like the rest of us in the wilderness of faith.

"Praise God!" he would shout over the phone. "Jesus is Lord, and all is well."

At first I felt envy rise and anger seethe. He flat ticked me off. But after a while I began to wonder, *What if this is real? What if he really is happy?* I finally decided to ask him, "OK, man. Don't you ever have bad days? Don't you ever go through trials and tribulations like the rest of us?"

"Well, Ed," he said, "I have feelings like everyone else, but I never really ask myself how I feel. I go to God and His Word and tell my feelings to line up with what God says." Then he started popcorning Bible verses at me.

I had read the verses he was quoting, but I had never hung on them as he was doing. I never thought I could cling to a Bible promise to alter how I felt. I thought my feelings were just what they were. I never imagined controlling them—I presumed that would be the domain of sovereignty.

GOD AND GORILLAS

"What does a five-hundred pound gorilla do?" the joke goes. "Anything he wants to," is the punch line. People think God is like that. He is the One with all the power. And everyone knows that insurance companies call the big stuff—hurricanes, earthquakes, floods, and tornadoes—"acts of God." Bad God days, I guess.

But is it fair to blame God for everything that happens on this planet? What about the devil? What does he do? Jesus once mentioned a tower falling on a bunch of tourists around Jerusalem (Luke 13:4), but he never mentioned God being involved—it appears to have been the result of bad construction. Could it be that humans are responsible for some things?

Yet there is a whole crowd that believes that everything that happens to them is predestined, which means you can't change stuff. No way. In the ancient world a group known as the Epicureans (the apostle Paul ran into these boys and girls in Acts 17) held to the idea that life was predetermined. Theirs was a philosophy of *determinism*—a fatalistic position. They reasoned that since we can change nothing, we might as well just float through life. "Don't worry; be happy," was their credo before Bobby McFerrin ever sang it. They encouraged imperturbability—don't get upset about things. They doled out the original "chill pill."

Before the fourth century, Christian thinkers didn't take determinism seriously. It was too pagan. It was the doctrine of life that pervaded the whole Roman Empire until Rome fell early in the fifth century. It is hard for Western moderns to appreciate the harshness of the ancient world. Life was cruel. War, death, plagues, exploding volcanoes, severe hardship, bad teeth (and no dentists or Tylenol), etc., were "givens" for those living in that day. Even with herculean effort, simple things like shelter and daily food were beyond the grasp of the average person. People died young.

In this kind of world, simply "holding up" through one's suffering was an amazing feat. Survival from one day (or hour) to the next was the focus for most. In this kind of helter-skelter, rough-and-tumble habitat, a philosophy of determinism, which gave the sense that someone or something was in charge, created a kind of emancipation of the mind from the fear of loss and dread—*maybe there is a higher purpose.* It was a seductive view.

Christianity stood in stark contrast to determinism. The idea of *grace* brought hope to humanity. Grace was the idea that God gets in the mix of the average person's world, and as a result, favor and good come into that person's life. Things *can* be different. The word *grace* comes from the Greek *charis*, a word used with a raised glass in the bars of ancient Greece to mean "the gods be with you." Its modern equivalent is "Have a good day." But the phrase was powerless—there are no *gods*. The Christian writers commandeered the word to mean God's unmerited favor, implying that "if God is with you, you really will have a good day!" Faith in God would actually bring change. No determinism here.

But determinism eventually found its way into Christian theology under the banner of sovereignty. By the Reformation, sovereignty became so inflated that people believed God even predetermines whether people go to heaven or hell—this is sovereignty on steroids and the radical emasculation of the human will.

QUE SERÁ, SERÁ

The problem with an overemphasis on God's sovereignty is that you end up with a kind of "que será, será" theology, rather than a biblical one. Some of you may remember the old song performed by Doris Day and written by Jay Livingston and Ray Evans. The chorus goes:

Que será será,
Whatever will be, will be.

Many today believe that whatever is to be, will be. We have nothing to do with the future; that is God's sphere. Things only happen, they contend, because of God's sovereignty, and human beings don't really *cause* anything to happen through prayer that God wouldn't have done anyway. Prayer for these folks is more of an aside, because God will do what God will do, irrespective of whether or not we pray. Therefore, one should pray simply to accept what God does, not to change what He does. Faith to such a believer is nothing more than agreement with what is already determined to be. The Bible highlights some who accepted this view.

When the religious leaders tried to stop the momentum of the burgeoning infant Church, one of their number wisely said, "So I am telling you: Hands off these men! Let them alone. If this program or this work is merely human, it will fall apart, but if it is of God, there is nothing you can do about it—and you better not be found fighting against God!" (Acts 5:38–39 MSG).

There are some "God things" we can do nothing about. They are just going to happen in our lives. Paul says God "works out everything in agreement with the counsel and design of his [own] will" (Eph. 1:11 AMP). He also wrote, "Who in the world do you think you are to second-guess God? Do you for one moment suppose any of us knows enough to call God into question? Clay doesn't talk back to the fingers that mold it, saying, 'Why did you shape me like this?'" (Rom. 9:20 MSG). God has this sovereign thing going on; we must accept that.

But the Bible is also jammed with story after story of God responding to the will of His people. Once, as Jesus walked through a crowd, a sick woman snuck up to him and touched the hem of his garment. The Bible says, "Jesus realized that power had gone out from him" (Mark 5:30). The woman was instantly healed. He stopped to investigate. When the woman came forward, trembling and admitting she had touched Him, He said something amazing. He told her that it was *her* faith that initiated the miracle. Think of that. A human being initiated an action of God.

Paul said God performs acts "prompted" by our faith (2 Thess. 1:11)! John boldly declares that "everyone who is born of God overcomes the world" and that "this is the victory that overcomes the world, even our faith" (1 John 5:4). This suggests that we don't have to wait for God to initiate everything He does on earth. If we learn to trust *on purpose*, we will see more of God's hand moving in our lives. Even a casual reading of Scripture points to the idea that things happen when we learn to trust and pray that don't happen if we don't.

There is a story in ancient Israel wherein a prophet tells the people facing an overwhelming foe that they will "not have to fight this battle" (2 Chron. 20:17). No casualties. God was going to fight for them. And He did. Another time an Israelite leader stood up as they faced a terrifying army and said, "Do not be afraid. Stand firm and you will see the deliverance the LORD will bring you today." But God replied to this leader, "Why are you crying out to me?" and commanded the leader and the people to engage and do some things for themselves (Ex. 14:13, 15). Sometimes God does it all; other times *we* have a role to play.

IS THE WILL FREE?

What *is* up to us? Is there anything contingent upon our actions? What rules or controls our lives here or in the hereafter? When we consider these haunting questions, we are trying to get our minds around whether or not God's involvement with us is *determined*—free from the influence of human will. On some level, we all feel the need to reconcile the contradistinctions between the idea of sovereign predestination and one's ability to choose his or her own destiny.

Admittedly, the whole "free will" thing has beguiled theologians and philosophers for thousands of years, and I am not about to say anything profound enough to settle it here, but perhaps that is the point. Perhaps there are some things that are determined and some that are not, some things that are destined to be and some that are not. Maybe we need wisdom and humility to discern which things fit where.

Take death, for example. The Bible says everyone is going to die (Heb. 9:27)—unless you are part of the group that is living when Jesus comes back. There is no way out—Sovereignty has spoken. Yet the Bible claims there are things you can do to add length to your life, like loving God's Word (Prov. 3:1–2).

An old, sick king named Hezekiah was told by a big-time, always-right prophet that he was going to die. The prophet then left the king's house.

Meanwhile, Hezekiah was bawling his eyes out, calling on God. God told the prophet, who had only gotten as far as the king's front yard, to go back and tell the king that God had just added fifteen years to his life (Isa. 38:5)! What was that all about? Somehow, God's sovereignty changed in response to a human action. Does free will play a role in death? Paul claimed that he had choice about the timing of his death (Phil. 1:22). I'm not suggesting this happens all the time, but it does happen *sometimes*, which means that, though death is determined, the timing sometimes isn't. Wow.

If death can be influenced by free will, what about life? What about the quality of our marriages and our relationships with our kids, friends, and coworkers? What about our career success or general well-being in life? How much do we control in all of this, and what does that control look like? How can we assert control without overstepping God's sovereignty?

So how can we know when things are to happen via sovereignty versus human will? More questions.

A SOVEREIGN PAUSE

In Genesis 1, a repeating pattern emerges: God *says* something, and it *happens*. His words are "magical." He says, "light," and it happens. He says, "water," and water appears. The same with land, sky, fish, birds, animals . . . and people. He speaks of them, and they become. There is no chance it might not happen. God didn't say, "Let there be light, but if that doesn't work, let there be . . . something else." In the creative gesture, light had no choice but to show up when God said so. God is sovereign.

But tell me if you don't think this is odd: when God comn
Adam *not* to do something—"You must not eat from the tree
knowledge of good and evil" (Gen. 2:17)— the Bible does *no* ~~ay,~~
"and it was so." In fact, after the command, God says Adam actually
has a choice. He can choose to go against God's command. If Adam
chooses to eat of the tree, the verse goes on to say, he will "surely die."
What? How could Adam have the choice to disobey an imperative of
the sovereign God? Light had no choice. Separation of land from
water had no choice. Nothing else in creation had choice. Why Adam?

Here's a maybe: *maybe* sovereignty always has preeminence until
it hits human will—then sovereignty *pauses*. Sovereignty doesn't dis-
appear; it just pauses until human *choice* has been made, and then it
kicks back in. Adam would live, as long as he didn't choose to eat of
that forbidden tree—sovereignty guaranteed it. But if he chose to
eat, then he would die—sovereignty guaranteed that too. God is
always sovereign, but maybe He is sovereign with *pause*, because He
respects and protects the thing that separates us from the rest of creation—our free will.

WHAT'S UNDER OUR CONTROL?

My friend Bruce was making choices I didn't even know a person
could make. His encouragement got me digging for Bible promises
and trusting God to do them in my life. My level of joy skyrocketed
as I prayed Scriptures like "The joy of the LORD is your strength"
(Neh. 8:10). Peace began to pervade my soul when I stopped and
intentionally thanked Jesus for promising "I am leaving you with a
gift—peace of mind and heart. And the peace I give isn't like the peace
the world gives. So don't be troubled or afraid" (John 14:27 NLT).

What if we can take more control of our emotions, our responses
to life, and even many of the negative circumstances that hit us,

through Bible-based praying and learning to trust God to help? What if everything is not determined?

Though it may be uncomfortable at the onset, the Bible supports the idea that what God does or does not do in our lives is directly connected to whether or not we trust Him. A pretty provocative thought. We have to face these questions: Am I really trusting God in my life? Am I trusting God in my finances? Do I trust Him in my marriage [or single life]? Do I really trust Him as I process life's vicissitudes? If we are *not*, it appears we cannot expect much in the way of God's activity in our lives.

In this view, much of life is under our individual control; it seems that the believer has an amazing amount of authority. But a number of questions immediately pop up when you think along these lines: What about sovereignty? What is God in control of? If I have this kind of authority, how do I feel about where my life is right now?

Presumably, if things are going well, you will feel pretty good. But what if things are going horribly? The idea that you are *totally* responsible for your own happiness or for how much good you experience can be a pretty heavy weight if your body is wracked with cancer, you have just lost your job, or your marriage is on the rocks.

If you uncritically accept that we have control in this world, you will end up believing that every person who has a hard life is a bad person. But is that really fair? Sadly, I think something in us wants to believe that, probably because if we can look at a person's pain and assign blame to him or her, it gives us the hope (false as it may be) that nothing bad like "that" will every happen to us, unless we do the same things we believe caused the problem.

But self-protecting judgments don't hold up when we face Bible stories like Job's. God says Job was "blameless and upright" (Job 1:1), and *yet* he was mugged by all kinds of horrible circumstances. Job's friends thought they understood why he was in torment and harped on him long about it. Though Job contended that he was not aware of any sin he had done to warrant his trouble, they repeatedly asserted that God only "repays a man for what he has done; he brings upon him what his conduct deserves" (Job 34:11). Job was confused, because he had done all he knew to do in the cause-and-effect world that he understood, but he still came up wanting. He had questions. Job's friends couldn't grasp complexity or paradox. They assumed Job had some sin he wasn't owning up to. But they were flat wrong. I have actually seen whole books written by groups desperate to protect their hyperfaith teachings, which lay out the *real* reasons behind Job's problems. (It appears Job has more friends than he realized.) Stories like his can get us confused about how much "authority" the believer really has.

The truth is, sometimes we have authority to stop things with our faith, but sometimes our faith helps us go through things we cannot stop. How can we tell the difference? I don't know. Faith is not an exact science. So what should we do? Simply this: know that with faith and good choices, you can have a great life—*most of the time.* So go for it. Seek God. Trust in Him to bring the best into your life. However, also realize that life in this world is way too complex (and you and I are too "creaturely") to think that our actions and responses in faith control *everything.*

I love trusting God for miracles of healing, provision, and restoration. But there are many who take this too far. They claim none of us would ever experience problems *if we had enough faith.* There are basic faith principles that, once mastered (and many believe they *have* mastered them), will allow one to eliminate all sickness, produce unlimited prosperity, and prevent all trouble.

The problem is, in the light of the testimony of Scripture and the history of God's people, the position is silly. All the "biggies" in the Bible (including Jesus) had trouble, contrary circumstances, and disappointment. Many faced illness, and there is no record that they were healed. Many were healed. Many prospered; but others were destitute. Yet the hyperfaith groups choose to believe in a kind of "victorious theology" that claims we can conquer anything *we* determine to be "bad" in this world. This is the "name-it-and-claim-it" crowd. This is the "I-can-have-whatever-I-want" crowd. This is the "God-has-to-do-what-I-want-Him-to-because-He-is-in-covenant-with-me" crowd.

PROBABILITY THEORY

In twenty-five-plus years of pastoral experience, I've come to believe that the odds are in your favor and you have the best shot at a happy life if you learn to do things right and trust God. The odds are greater that your marriage will be wonderful if you fight to have a godly marriage and trust God. The odds are that you will live long and see good days. *But there are no absolute guarantees.* Faith is more like probability theory. Ask a scientist where an atom's electron is at any given moment and she will tell you where it *probably* is—most of the time. Trust God in life and things will *probably* get better for you—most of the time. But sometimes they don't get better. In fact, sometimes things get worse. In other words, *bad things happen to good people.*

People who say having "great faith" guarantees that one will never suffer are either too ignorant, too young, too inexperienced, or too isolated from real people. They have definitely joined the "Beyond the Bible" club. Some of the godliest people I know have had some pretty horrible moments. Sometimes life is logical; sometimes it isn't. And when it is not, you have to "fly" by faith, trusting that God is good—good enough to work out the bad.

There is a story in the life of King David that illustrates this point. He hears that his son has taken ill and begins to fast and pray night and day that the child will be healed. But the child dies. Because of David's intense vigil, his servants are afraid that he might do "some-

thing desperate." So they don't tell him. But David sees them wh[i]
pering and asks if the child is dead. When he learns the truth, the
Bible says David gets up, washes and gets dressed, worships at the
temple for a while, and then returns to his house and asks to be
served some food. His servants are confused. "Why are you acting
this way?" they ask. "While the child was alive, you fasted and wept,
but now that the child is dead, you get up and eat!" (2 Sam. 12:21).

David responds, "While the child was still alive, I fasted and wept.
I thought, 'Who knows? The LORD may be gracious to me and let
the child live.' But now that he is dead, why should I fast? Can I bring
him back again? I will go to him, but he will not return to me" (vv.
22–23).

This is how I think the believer should respond to trouble. When
it comes, we hit it with prayer, faith, fasting, crying, and a total abandonment to God and His promises. Sometimes that changes the
world. Sometimes it doesn't. If it doesn't, we need to get up, wash
and change clothes, go to church and worship, and grab a bite to eat.
We move on. And the next time trouble knocks, we go after it again.

Why is this so critical? Because if we are not careful, we end up
harshly and unfairly judging people who have trouble. Why do you
think hurting people often run from church? Just talk with families
whose churches preach healing and miracles, but who *still* lost loved
ones to cancer. Ask them how they were treated after the death of
their mom or dad or brother or sister. Ask if they thought the
church was loving and fair in their assessment of things after the
tragic events. It's easy to see someone in trouble or experiencing
hardship and piously judge why, when we have no clue why. We
quickly become like Job's "friends"—who were so *un*friendly.

Though the Bible is clear that trust in God can dramatically impact
our lives, it is equally clear that there is mystery in life—things happen
that we cannot get our minds around. In those times we have to learn
to dance with the mystery. We have to be OK with questions. We

need to do what we know to do, but at the end of the day, we must trust our sovereign God for the outcome.

Obviously, this kind of chatter musters a boatload of questions. I was a fundamentalist once. We didn't have any questions, only answers. I think we thought asking questions was a sign of a lack of faith. But hooray for questions. Questions help us understand the seeming contradictions present in faith. Authentic Christianity is lived out in the tension of paradox. Questioning is the only way to stay balanced in the tension—it is the pole in the hands of the tightrope walker. Ask questions. Maybe Christianity isn't just about having answers; maybe it's about asking questions; maybe it's about being OK—trusting even—when the questions remain unanswered. At least for now.

10

hermen's disease:
things are not as they appear

T he abomination that causes desolation'?" (Matt. 24:15), Jim read aloud. Then he looked up and asked, "What in the world is that?"

We were all pretty new at Bible interpretation, but we had decided to wrestle through the prophetic Bible verses on the end times. And it was a free-for-all.

A couple of us took a stab at possible meanings for "the abomination that causes desolation." No one even suggested we look at the historical or textual contexts in which the verse was nestled. We tried to figure out what it meant through our eyeglasses of modernity.

A guy who was visiting our group for the first time piped right in. "The Lord has shown me what this means." (It's always a little more interesting when God weighs in on an interpretation.)

We all looked at him with anticipation.

"I've discovered that it is helpful to break words apart when you study Scripture," he purported with all seriousness. "If you break down 'abomination,' you get *a-bom-in-nation*. This verse is a prediction that a number of nations would one day get the *atomic bomb*. And it's happening," he exclaimed with lots of excitement. "We are in the last days!"

HERMEN-*WHO?*

A *hermeneutic* is a method or principle we use to interpret truth. It helps us determine the meaning of what is going on around us. For example, in the premodern world a violent natural event like an earthquake or exploding volcano was viewed as some kind of vengeance from the gods. That was their hermeneutic. Gods do that sort of thing. When there was a natural disaster, people assumed someone had killed a sacred animal or committed some heinous crime that angered the gods, and the cataclysmic event was retribution for that immoral act. In the modern world, we know natural disasters brew because of a number of very natural conditions. That is our hermeneutic. What premoderns saw as acts of the gods, moderns see as the logical result of nature's adjustments. No vengeance here.

A different hermeneutic leads to a different interpretation.

The hermeneutics we use provide a framework for processing data, as prescription eyeglasses "frame" what we (who need them) see. I remember getting my first pair of glasses as a kid and being amazed at how it helped me see the world in a whole new way—clearly. I had become used to the blur.

In my small hometown in rural Wisconsin, I knew a lady who believed there was no way the United States ever got those men on the moon—not really. When asked about the live television broadcasts that captured the event, she would say, "It was all Hollywood. They staged the whole thing. It was fake, and a bunch of people made a lot of money from our tax dollars."

Her hermeneutic "glasses" made the whole thing appear as a hoax. She lived with a "conspiracy" hermeneutic.

Viewing the world as conspiratorial or interpreting biblical prophecy by breaking the English words apart (especially since Scripture was originally written in Hebrew and Greek) are examples of bad hermeneutics. When you use faulty methods or tools to interpret something, the world will end up looking distorted and weird, not unlike trying to wear someone else's glasses—it will give you a headache.

Sadly, there are some bizarre hermeneutics out there. These distort the world of truth and give people lots of headaches. And there is no place where this is truer than in the context of religion. When it comes to what we believe about God (theology), how we think He wants us to live (doctrines), what we can or cannot do (commandments and injunctions), etc., Christians have so many different sets of glasses, we make Elton John's eyewear collection seem paltry.

All kinds of things influence the way we see things: our experiences, our parents, Dr. Phil, our friends, the churches we've attended, *The Matrix*, our prejudices, expectations, hopes, failures, God, the devil, being American, an *Oprah* show we once saw—these all color the way we interpret our world and our faith. They color our hermeneutic, and we get "Hermen's disease."

BLUBLOCKER HERMENUETICS

Back in the '80s there was a huge promotion for BluBlocker sunglasses. They boasted of providing UV and blue-light protection for the eyes. I sported a pair of those unisex "As seen on TV" sunglasses with a large degree of misguided pride (you should see the pictures!).

One day my family and I were heading out of town and we stopped to fill up with gas and grab some treats from the quick mart. Gail asked me to get her some of her favorite gum. I always recognized her gum by the color of the package. She liked the Wriggles kind in the big blue pack. I grabbed it, paid, and brought it back to the car.

We were heading down the road when she asked, "Why didn't you get me my regular kind?"

"I did," I answered.

"No, you didn't," she said as she pointed to the pack.

I took the gum, held it up, and said rather sarcastically, "Gail, the pack is blue. This is the kind you like!"

She paused for a second and said, "Take off the BluBlockers, Eddie."

I reached up and pulled off the glasses and realized I had inadvertently purchased the green gum, thinking I was purchasing the blue gum. The BluBlockers made the green pack look blue.

That's what happens to us. Our lives are "colored" by our experience, and we interpret our surroundings uncritically. That means what looks true sometimes isn't, and what looks untrue is sometimes true. All of us have some BluBlocker hermeneutics going on at some level. Our ideas, presuppositions, and even prejudices color our reasoning and interpretive skills. We don't see clearly.

THE GOOD BOOK

I love the Bible. It is a book full of narrative history, genealogies, laws, poetry, proverbs, prophetic oracles, riddles, drama, biographical sketches, parables, letters, sermons, and apocalypses.

I want to say it's magical, but some of my evangelical brothers and sisters would get nervous. It is definitely a mystical book that fills the believing heart with life, wonder, grace, power, and comfort. All believers treasure the Bible. It has been the best seller in the world since printing began. When the Gutenberg press was invented, the first words it reproduced were the words of the Bible.

However, I think we have done a disservice to people by giving them the impression that the Bible is easy. We imply that it's easy to understand and easy to apply. But that's like saying marriage is easy. Certainly marriage can be wonderful, but it is *not* easy. It is not easy to keep your "I" on your spouse and off yourself. It is not easy for men to understand women, and vice versa. The same is true for the Bible. Understanding it is often very difficult. There are texts that seem impossible to comprehend. That is why, throughout history, so many have misused the Bible in so many horrible ways.

It is hard to imagine, but the sacred Scriptures, which have brought unspeakable comfort and blessing to countless millions, have been used to bring pain, horror, and death to many. The Bible was used to justify the instruments used on "heretics" (the Christians who disagreed with the Christians who were in charge) during the Inquisition. Christian leaders used iron collars with spikes to impale the throats of those who opposed them, as well as stretching machines that tore people apart—in the name of God, of course.

Throughout history, the Bible has been used to defend violence against racial minorities, women, Jews, abortionists, and homosexuals.

On a less destructive but equally ridiculous note, believers throughout history have used the Bible to "prove" specifically *when* Jesus Christ would return. I guess Jesus never got the memo.

When faced with the possibility of war, one group has used Scripture to prove we should go to war, while the group on the other side of the ideological aisle used the same Bible to prove we are *never* supposed to go to war.

How can this be? How can there be such divergent thought about the truth?

BluBlockers.

Some would argue that the Bible doesn't need "interpretation," and for many texts that is true—they just need to be obeyed. Paul commands, "Do everything without complaining or arguing" (Phil. 2:14). That doesn't need interpretation; it needs obedience, plain and simple.

But not all texts are that simple. And if we are not careful, we will think our understanding of what we read is the understanding that the Holy Spirit intended. But that is a huge assumption, and it ignores the fact that our experiences, the culture we live in, and prior understanding of words and ideas always inject themselves into what we read. We are kidding ourselves if we think our unseen biases cannot lead us astray and cause us to read unintended ideas into the text. We have to come to grips with the fact that the gum isn't always blue, even if it looks that way to us.

TATTOOS AND BODY PIERCING

Let's say you grew up believing that it is wrong for people to get tattoos and have their body pierced. Maybe you heard your mom and dad say it was wrong. Or perhaps it's because, when you were growing up, tattoos and body piercing were only fashionable for mean-looking bikers, biker chicks, and those on the short end of the socioeconomic scale. Is that an unfair prejudice? Yeah. But if that was your experience, it impacts how you think.

Whatever the reason, inbred opinions cause us to read Bible texts with a predetermined *selectivity*—some texts literally pop off the page at us, while others remain completely ignored.

We come across a verse like, "Do not cut your bodies . . . or put tattoo marks on yourselves. I am the LORD" (Lev. 19:28) and it leaps off the page to us. And when an internal "resonance" occurs, it can feel very much like a spiritual epiphany—like the voice of God. *No wonder tattoos and piercings trouble us so,* we reason. *God feels the same way!*

Never mind that in the previous verse men are told, *never* "cut the hair at the sides of your head or clip off the edges of your beard" (Lev. 19:27). We ignore that. But if we choose to obey the command that forbids tattoos or piercings on the basis of God's Word, we must by necessity of reason demand that men grow side-whiskers and scraggly, untrimmed beards—with a great big "Praise the Lord!"

So why aren't we fair and reasonable with Bible texts like these?

Because something in us longs to emphasize the verses that resonate with our own opinions and biases, while ignoring the ones that don't. However, it's one thing to interpret things in a biased, squirrelly way; it's quite another to slap God's endorsement on our interpretation. But people do it every day.

We don't need to do that. If we don't like something, we just need to be honest about it. Gail and I do not personally like tattoos or body piercing. As our four kids grew, we told them tattoos and piercings were not allowed in the Gungor house. We said with a smile on our faces, "It isn't that God is against it—in fact, he has tattoos. He has *us* tattooed on His hand. [See Isa. 49:16 AMP.] Apparently, He's *into* tattoos. It's that your mom and dad are against it. We don't want you permanently altering your body until you are an adult and decide to do so. We're just weird, old-fashioned parents. Get used to it."

We think it's OK for parents to be uptight about some stuff. Parents have the right to be weird. We just can't put those weirdnesses on God and swear "by heaven" (James 5:12). If you do so, you ultimately risk driving your kids away from God.

Be weird. Just own it.

THE CURE

My friend Rex is colorblind. Anytime he picks out his own clothes, people stare. When he drives, he must be extra careful—he can't distinguish the red lights from the green. When I found out, I was surprised. I had never noticed, and I had known him for years.

When I mentioned how well he concealed his sight challenge, he said, "That's because I don't trust myself. If I did, you would have known it the day you met me—I would have been the one dressed like a clown. But I learned early that if I don't ask for help, I'm in trouble."

We need to get past our own BluBlocker presuppositions, which we've picked up from our families, our churches, our socioeconomic status, and the good and bad experiences we've endured. The first step to doing so is to *not* trust ourselves. Then we can approach biblical interpretation with more humility and suspicion.

It takes a tremendous amount of humility to accept that we don't see everything clearly. Human pride does not like to accept the suspicion that there may be a dark undertow to our reasoning processes. It is hard to accept that we cannot trust ourselves. But we live a lie if we do not unmask the depth of our pretensions and prejudices and admit that it is impossible to live in a fallen world without that fallenness impacting our reasoning at some level.

Seventeenth century mathematician Blaise Pascal once wrote, "Truly it is an evil to be full of faults, but it is a still greater evil to be unwilling to recognize them."[1] We must recognize our inclination to *believe* that we think clearly and accurately. We are all colorblind. The Scripture says that we are fools if we are uncritical about our thinking—we must actively pursue outside input and assessment (Prov. 12:15).

We can't trust ourselves; we must ask for help—from God and others. This is why the psalmist cried out, "Search me, O God, and know my heart; test me and know my anxious thoughts. See if there is any offensive way in me, and lead me in the way everlasting" (Ps. 139:23–24).

COMMON SENSE

The second way to arrest the negative effects of Hermen's disease is to approach the Scriptures with common sense. Remember that the Bible is a divine library filled with history, law, poetry, songs, stories, letters, parables, drama, philosophy, sermons—and more. Don't try to interpret every word, thinking that God gave us His Word just so we can *dissect* it. He didn't. Paul said Scripture is literally God's *breath* (2 Tim. 3:16). It is alive (Heb. 4:12). Much of it is simply to be experienced.

We moderns are driven to use analysis as the chief weapon in our intellectual arsenal. But we often make it the *only* one. That is problematic. Analysis yields wonderful things, but not *all* the truth.

We used to have a dog named Max. If I wanted you to know what he was like (Max is dead), I could send his remains for you to dissect, poke, and examine under a microscope. You would learn a lot about Max that way. But the analysis wouldn't let you know his personality or how many tricks he could do or how he interacted with the different members of our family or how scared he got the night he ran into the back end of a skunk.

Truth is like that. You can learn a lot by dissecting it, but you can't get the whole of it by cutting it up into the original Greek and Hebrew words. You can't get the real picture by analyzing the verb syntax or the sentence structure. It is arguable that analysis is the slenderest part of discovering biblical truth.

When you approach the Scriptures, don't just try to analyze. Sitting down with the Bible is like a visit with Jesus. It gives you His thoughts on life and will reveal wonderful secrets about how God wants you to live and relate to Him and others. Look and listen for the universal principles of Scripture.

As you read, try to accomplish the following:

A. Read and study with an open heart. A few moments in prayer before your study time will help ensure an open, honest heart.

B. Be open to changing the way you think as you read the Bible. When you read the Bible, you will see God's point of view on various subjects, such as money, family life, ethical choices, etc. Decide to change if you have believed something else.

C. Keep the context in mind. The three types of context are:

Verse context – Consider the verses that precede and follow the one you are studying. Many people pull verses right out of their setting and create or support wrong ideas.

Passage context – Always look at a passage in the light of others addressing the same subject. Make sure you have at least two or three verses that say the same thing before you begin to accept a truth.

Historical context – Take time to research and consider the time in history when the text was written and the unique circumstances surrounding that text.

D. Always ask yourself four basic questions as you study:

1. *Who is being spoken to?* (Sometimes the "wicked man" is being addressed, which is the person who lacks interest in serving God. Don't take onto yourself what is said about him. Because of your relationship with Jesus, you are called righteous [2 Cor. 5:21]. Bible verses that address "the righteous" or the "righteous man" *do* refer to you.)
2. *What is being said?*
3. *What does it mean to those present when it was spoken?*
4. *How do I apply it practically in my life?*

SOME GENERAL ENCOURAGEMENTS

Be a student. A great number of study helps are available in bookstores and online to help one steer safely into a clearer biblical understanding. Search some of these out. Try some different Bible translations. Always remember, there are lots of spiritual weirdos, so try to study writers who stay close to doctrines that have survived for centuries. Be especially wary of people who say, "God told me this means . . ." God *may* have spoken to them, but you should test what they say (1 Thess. 5:21). The Bible says, "there is nothing new under the sun" (Eccl. 1:9). If God told *them,* then He has told others also. Make sure trusted "others" throughout history say the same thing.

Be OK with tension. The Bible has paradox. A paradox is a seemingly contradictory statement that is nonetheless true. The Bible is chock-full of these, and it creates tension. Jesus taught that if we want to live, we must die. If we wish to receive, we must give away. If we want to be free, we must become slaves. The Bible teaches of the Trinity—God in three persons. God is one, and yet He is three.

Enjoy the paradox.

Don't try to resolve all the mysteries in Scripture. Enjoy them. Let's face it: some verses just don't make sense. What, for instance, did Paul mean when he alluded to the Corinthians baptizing "for the dead" (1 Cor. 15:29)? *What was that?* If we ask and study and ponder and still don't come up with an answer, I think we need to be OK with not figuring it out. All the parts that I *don't get,* I relegate to the idea that "the secret things belong to the LORD" (Deut. 29:29).

Faith is supposed to have *mystery* in it. Paul penned, "Now to him who is able to do immeasurably more than all we ask or imagine . . ." (Eph. 3:20).

When you run into principles, analogies, stories, or events, in the Bible that are mysterious, smile. Be satisfied with not knowing exactly what is going on. I'm not saying to not try to figure it out, but after you try and still come up empty, chill. Be OK with God being in charge.

Watch out! When I drive, I drive suspiciously. I am suspicious that I may crash, so I don't reach cruising speed, put on the cruise control, and read a book—I watch the road. I am suspicious that other drivers may run into me, so I drive defensively. When I read the

97

Bible, I am suspicious of my own hermeneutic bias, so I try to be humble and watchful. I use the tools I list above.

History is full of examples of people using biblical texts to justify the denigration or persecution or disenfranchising of others—while carrying the implication that the ones using these texts are the true bearers of the uncompromised Word of God. *Watch out.* We need to approach the Scriptures with a suspicion that we will always be tempted to default to the forbidden "private interpretation" (2 Peter 1:20 KJV).

We need to challenge each other's hermeneutics—to question things more; to use common sense; to point out how opinions predispose us to judgments, and how prejudice, closed mindedness, and bigotry invariably produce a diseased hermeneutic. I always go to DEF CON 1 status whenever I hear a televangelist or Christian friend say, "The Lord showed me that this verse means . . ." and then proceed to tell me something that doesn't stand up against common sense. More often than not, it isn't the Lord at all—it's the person's own diseased hermeneutic self.

So beware—of Hermen's disease.

11

last-days flu: the sky is falling

When I first came to Christ, the group I hung with talked a lot about the return of Jesus Christ. We used to pass out fake newspapers with the headline "Christ Returns!" We were sure the event known as "the Rapture" (where Jesus returns to snatch away His followers) was *close*—certainly within the next year or two. That was a little more than thirty-five years ago.

But last-days prophecy stuff is fascinating and extremely motivating. Thinking about the possible imminent return of Jesus produces amazing commitment and devotion. The apostle John said a person who thinks about it "purifies himself, just as he is pure" (1 John 3:3). The whole idea that we are going to see Jesus is very cool. No longer living by faith—we're *really* going to see Him!

But there are problems.

As far back as you care to go historically, you can find preachers with a penchant for interpreting Bible prophecy by holding the daily news in one hand and the Bible in the other. Using obscure texts and arbitrary methods, many have tried to prove the identity of the Antichrist or discern which country is the nation known as "Magog" in Scripture (a nation important in last-days prophecy).

Back in the 1950s, many last-days pundits claimed Magog was the Soviet Union, but in the 1980s the Union collapsed. Then new revelations began to come as to the identity of "true" Magog (many now say Magog is Islam).

What confuses me is how the last-days experts talk with such confidence and authority. They don't "suggest" this or that may happen or that a verse *might* mean this or that—it is a done deal; their interpretation is absolute truth. And something is always happening in the Middle East or elsewhere that serves as another indication that the return of Jesus is *just around the corner.*

The other day I heard a well-meaning Bible-prophecy radio minister try to use a very cryptic Bible text to prove that a recent series of terrorist attacks in Israel were specifically predicted in Scripture! These guys read the *New York Times* and the *Jerusalem Post* the way a psychic reads tea leaves. And with a rising fever in the air, you get the feeling you need to stay close and stay tuned to hear the latest from their prophetic perspective. You want to make sure you are ready.

But then, when what they say doesn't happen or the interpretation they have been espousing demands adjustment, they do so as unapologetically and frequently as the local meteorologist. But are Bible prophecies supposed to be approached like weather forecasts, or should we just be a little more tentative about our interpretations to begin with?

KNOCK, KNOCK; WHO KNOWS?

If you want to take a trip to a foreign country, just start reading the Bible passages that describe the last days, which you find in books like Ezekiel, Daniel, Zechariah, and Isaiah—but especially in the book of Revelation. You run into angels, trumpets, earthquakes, biting locusts with human-faced heads, beasts, dragons, and bottomless pits. Alice's Wonderland looks tame by comparison.

Why is there so much room for arbitrary interpretation in the arena of Bible prophecy? Primarily because most of it is written in a style that isn't found anywhere else in modern literature, and we have a hard time trying to decipher it. It's called apocalyptic literature.

In Bible days there were dozens of apocalypses that were popular with Jews and Christians (not all were considered canonical, of course). Apocalyptic literature is just that, a genre of literature. Just as stories, parables, and psalms have specific literary characteristics, so does an apocalypse.

Imagine being part of an archaeological team one million years from now that uncovers a few "knock, knock" jokes from our century. Let's say you have no counterpart in your culture—no "knock, knock" jokes exist.

You translate the text:

Knock, knock.
Who's there?
Duane.
Duane who?
Duane the bathtub, I think I'm duowning.

As you try to interpret the writing, someone suggests, "Perhaps the word *knock* has some kind of special meaning. Notice they said it twice."

Someone else pipes in and says, "Yes, and apparently Duane is the name of a bathing device—it reads, 'Duane the bathtub.'"

Yet another remarks, "And what do you think 'duowning' is?"

"Perhaps it has something to do with the double 'knock,'" you reply.

You all miss the point.

You might come up with half a dozen equally ridiculous interpretations simply because you don't get the fact that this is a joke. Jokes have characteristics that must be understood in order for the joke to make sense. The same kind of thing is true when we are reading apocalyptic literature. Apocalyptic literature has certain characteristics that must be mastered for this kind of literature to make any sense to us.

Characteristics of apocalyptic literature include heavy themes of judgment and salvation; they come jammed with visions and dreams, and the language is cryptic and symbolic; the images within an apocalypse are often forms of fantasy rather than reality; and time and events are neatly divided and carefully ordered with a great fondness for the symbolic use of numbers.

When you take a book like Revelation that is populated with visions, dreams, cryptic and symbolic language, fantasy, some general epistle or letter material, and a huge chunk of specific prophetic elements, you have the makings of a right gnarly piece of literature.

But most of us ignore all that and approach prophetic texts with an open heart and prayer. It sounds good—spiritual even. But is it? Go ahead and put one hundred people in a room and ask them to run at this kind of material prayerfully, with an open heart, and you will end up with one hundred thousand different interpretations.

As I pointed out in Chapter 10, not all Scripture is easy to understand. And we are kidding ourselves if we think our interpretations are not influenced by our theological heritage, ecclesiastical traditions, cultural norms, and life experiences. This should make us very suspicious of our understanding as we read Scriptures. This is especially true when reading prophetic segments.

For example, if you think God directed Bible prophecy toward Americans more than Libyans, Afghans, or Sudanese, then end-times verses will read differently to you. Europeans and Americans tend to hold the Bible in one hand and Western newspapers in the other to discern where we are on the prophetic "tick-tock."

But if you are a brother or sister in Christ from the Sudan (many who are currently having their property seized and their children taken from them), you may think the Great Tribulation is taking place *now*, and you have already met the armies of the Antichrist.

We need to be more wary of our last-days interpretations.

MOTIVATED TO SERVE

Something about the return of Jesus Christ gets people motivated to serve. But I would suggest the motivation is not good when we get people excited about the return of Christ based on current events that are interpreted hastily and inappropriately.

In 1988 a book came out titled something like *88 Reasons Why the Rapture Is in 1988*. Tens of thousands of believers bought that little book and made it a central issue in their lives.

People I knew were passing the books out to relatives, friends, coworkers, and neighbors. It created quite a stir. I had been around the block a couple of times by 1988, so I wasn't nearly as taken with the idea. I remember sharing with those I pastored at the time, "Don't get too excited, folks. Jesus said no one would know the exact time or hour of His return! I hate to pop your end-times bubble, but I have some plans for 1989."

When Jesus didn't come back, the author came out with another work with a title to the tune of *89 Reasons Why the Rapture Is in 1989*. It didn't sell nearly as well.

People who got all jacked up by that book were disappointed and embarrassed after Jesus didn't return in 1988. Some even slipped away from the Lord. Why? I think talking about Jesus's return the way Chicken Little did when he said, "The sky is falling," always yields less-than-favorable results. It's weird. Last-days fever is contagious. Chicken Little always seems to meet up with Henny Penny, Cocky Locky, and Goosey Poosey, and then you really have a mess. It turns into a whole last-days movement.

Trying to motivate people to serve God by using fabricated time-lines on Rapture dates and presenting them like a salesperson's "last-chance" sale always produces a short-term yield. This kind of motivation is like a flu bug—you get hit hard, but it only lasts a little while. And when it's over, you feel worn out.

A HEALTHY ESCHATOLOGY

When you read the New Testament, you get the idea that they expected Jesus to return at any moment—*and that was two thousand years ago!* Why would they talk about the return of Jesus in a way that suggested it could happen at any moment? I think the answer is found in Paul's comment that God rewards those "who have longed for his appearing" (2 Tim. 4:8). God wants us to think about, dream about, and long for the return of Jesus Christ.

Honestly, until very recently I never did that. I never consciously fostered a longing for the appearing of Jesus. When I first came to Him and heard the end-times message, I got excited and was motivated by it—but Jesus never came. And because many of the events that were used to prove that His return was imminent proved no such thing, I got a tad jaded.

Today, I don't believe our "longing" for the return of Jesus should be based on forcing obscure texts into modern news stories. I think it should be based on the fact that earth isn't home. Jesus told us before He left, "Do not let your hearts be troubled" (John 14:1). He said, "I am going . . . to prepare a place for you" (v. 2). Then He said, "I will come back and take you . . . with me that you also may be where I am" (v. 3).

This planet is not home for us. At best, it is a hotel room. Our longing for the return of Jesus needs to rest in the fact that He has made a home for us and is coming to get us—not based on some prophecy expert's dubious revelation. It is said of the saints of old, "they were longing for a better country—a heavenly one. Therefore God is not ashamed to be called their God, for he has prepared a city for them" (Heb. 11:16).

Next time you feel a little out of sorts because life is less than you had hoped, look up and grin. This is not your home. This is not heaven. But heaven is coming to get you. And instead of running to something inappropriate (viz, sin) to quench the inner cry that only Jesus can satisfy, tell the Lord, "I am so achy for heaven. I am longing for Jesus to come and get me out of here—Jesus, I long for Your appearing. Though there is good here, nothing completely satisfies—nothing but You. If You don't come physically right now, at least come to me spiritually and nourish my weary heart!" This simple prayer can help you keep your heart pure and bring you to a whole new level spiritually.

Don't be sick with "last-days flu"—instead, live *well* in the *last days.*

12

spiritual elephantiasis:
let's make this spectacular

Elephantiasis is a vivid and accurate term for the actual medical syndrome it describes: the visible enlargement of the arms, legs, or genitals to elephantine size. It is caused by parasites known as *filariae,* or *filarial worms*. These long, threadlike worms block the body's lymphatic system and causes fluids to collect in the tissues, which leads to swelling. Limbs can swell so enormously that they resemble an elephant's foreleg in size, texture, and color. This is a severely disfiguring and disabling condition.

I think it's possible to contract a kind of spiritual "elephantiasis." It comes when we embrace a "wormy" thought: *If it's really God, it has to be big—it has to be spectacular.* This thought wiggles its way into our egos, our expectations, and our planning—and they become *enormous*. We then sustain huge egos, gargantuan expectations, and a plan that sounds reasonable only to a madman.

Just talk to a handful of believers who really want to shake the world for God. At least one or two will have dreams that are big— really *big*. They will tell you, "I don't know all the details, but it's going to be *big*." But if you press them, they will share the details they *do* know: it will involve millions of people, millions of dollars, and, of course, a private jet.

In the diseased American church, you can't grow up to be a fireman or an at-home mom—not if you want to change the world.

We charismatics are notorious for wanting *big*. We have big ideas. Big ministries. Big hair. Just look at how some of us pray for people at the altars. No gentle, quiet praying there. We yell. We flail our arms and extend our palms. We push people down. We like things big—elephant-sized, really.

A VISITATION

When I first began pastoring twenty-five years ago, I spent the bulk of my time studying, praying, and counseling people. I lived and breathed ministry and longed for the spectacular. Whatever was going to happen, I knew it was going to be large. My ego, my expectations, and my plans grew exponentially by the minute. And I could almost hear the jet God was sending my way.

Though I loved my family with all my heart, I had a difficult time justifying "casual" time with them. "After all," I'd reason, "people are going to hell, and I need to stay close to God. I can't get too tangled up with everyday things."

My greatest dread was my "day off." That was a day I was to stay home and do the regular stuff—non-big stuff. Although Gail looked forward to these days, they were like a scourge to me. I would rather be praying, preparing, and setting strategies to affect the world-at-large than taking out the trash, tumbling on the floor with our toddler, or going hunting at the mall with Gail. On those days, I would often exasperate her because, though I was with her physically, she sensed that I was somewhere else mentally and emotionally. I was tons of fun.

I knew God expected me to "service" my relationship with my family, and I really loved them. But it seemed to me that God valued ministry over garbage removal, playtime, and casual chatter—and

He certainly didn't care about shopping. There was never any question that if someone needed me to pray, counsel, or preach at him, I must lay my day off "on the altar" to follow God's call.

Then came the day in the spring of 1982 that would forever change the way I saw things.

I woke up late that morning and didn't get my regular prayer and study time in before the family was up and about. I knew that if I ran off to study and pray then, it would look to Gail like another workday. So I stayed home and started participating in what was happening around the house—though I was disappointed and a little short on patience for not getting my devotional time.

I kept mentally beating myself, thinking, *I should have gotten up earlier! How can I expect to win the world for Christ if I am not consistent in my devotional time?*

Then I would catch myself: *Forget it for now, Edwin. You're supposed to focus on family stuff for now—you can pray later.*

By noon I had helped clean the house; had coffee and conversation with Gail; and fed, changed, and started rocking Michael, our firstborn, to sleep for his midday nap. Gail also decided to take a nap. As the nap window opened, I smelled opportunity. I thought to myself, *All right! I can run and spend some time with the Lord.*

Actually, by this time in the day I was somewhat proud of myself. I had been a pretty good husband and father all morning, and now I was ready to press in and be a good Christian *too!*

After Michael fell asleep, I laid him down and hastened toward the stairs, excited that I could finally work in my God time. As I passed our bedroom, I heard Gail call to me, "Honey, would you please rub the back of my neck?" She had a headache.

My reaction wasn't good. I bristled inside. *Doesn't she appreciate all I've done today?* I thought. *I'm a pastor . . . a spiritual leader . . . God's man. I need time with God!*

I knew she had the right to ask for attention, but this wasn't the right time. I had fulfilled my natural duties all day long. It was time to me to be about my Father's business.

Just as I was about to protest, I felt the Lord say to me, *If you'll do this, I will show you something.*

I was immediately puzzled. I usually had to wait before God in prayer for some time before I would get the slightest impression, much less hear words. Here I was in the midst of frustration and feeling selfish about my life, and He was clearly speaking. "OK," I said to Him. Then I walked, somewhat bewildered, into our room and sat on the bed.

As I began to massage Gail's neck, something happened that I had not expected—the very presence of God filled our room. Thoughts raced in different directions through my mind, *What's happening? Am I going to have a vision? Does she sense this? Why are You present like this, Lord?*

Then, as I looked at Gail, she seemed more beautiful than ever. This presence seemed to make me appreciate my wife more! I loved just being with her and rubbing her neck. It seemed important and valuable. I had been heading for study and prayer. *Surely* that was more important in God's eyes than spending more time with the girl I had married . . . or was it? What was going on?

There is a concept in the Bible known as the "anointing." The term *anointed* implies an "upon" presence of the Holy Spirit. "Upon" suggests the idea of pressure from above. The *anointing* is an action of God wherein He comes upon individuals and they are enabled or empowered to do things they could not have done without Him. The anointing not only affects the anointed one, but it also releases power to change those who are ministered to while under its influence.

I was familiar with God's presence, or anointing, at various places in my life. As a preacher, I often sensed His presence as I spoke. In counseling sessions, a wave of insight would come, and I knew it was God equipping me to give godly counsel. Many times, when praying for sick or troubled people, I have sensed a strong anointing of God, which has emboldened my faith for more effective prayer. As I have witnessed about my faith to others, I have experienced God's palpable presence that helped me say things I didn't plan to say or even realized I knew. But I had never experienced God's presence or *anointing* to be a husband. I thought I was to do that alone! I never imagined God cared about something so domestic.

On that day with Gail, the Holy Spirit was "anointing" me, enabling me to be sensitive to my wife's needs.

But it was more than that.

I knew I was supposed to be sensitive to her needs before experiencing this anointing. At Bible school they taught me it was necessary to keep your home in order if you wanted to be useful to God in ministry. Keeping one's home relationships in line was an obligation—like flossing your teeth or changing the oil in your car.

The unusual thing here was that *God* was anointing me to do something everyday, something totally common. He was anointing me to meet my wife's needs just as He had always anointed me to preach the gospel or minister to hurting people. That said to me that God cares about my life—my boring, mundane, everyday, nonbig life. That changed *everything* for me. I began to see that my everyday life was not just the stuff of duty; it qualified to be in the arena of *adventure*!

Because of its importance to me, the ministry has forever been a thrill. I always experience a deep sense of purpose and satisfaction when I sense God's presence touching others through me. It has never been a dull or boring thing to follow God. It has been an adventure.

Home life, on the other hand, seemed pretty mundane by comparison. It had always been part of the "daily grind" of responsibility. But my whole viewpoint changed that afternoon. For God to speak to me in such a dramatic way made me realize that it was a very important area to Him. I saw that everyday life didn't belong in the domain of the ordinary and the not-so-important, but it was to be on the same level of importance as reaching the world for Jesus. My natural life could be made *super*, making it *super*natural. I realized I had so longed for the spectacular that I had missed the *super*natural.

There is an enablement, or anointing, for us as spouses, parents, children, employees, employers, and so on. God doesn't just move in big plans or with worldwide schemes. We need His anointing in our everyday relationships as desperately as we need His anointing to reach out to the world-at-large.

The God who said, "Go into all the world and preach the good news to all creation" (Mark 16:15) is the same one who said, "Husbands love your wives" (Eph. 5:25) and "be kind . . . to one another" (Eph. 4:32). We don't have to destroy or neglect our relationships with family and friends to serve God in ministry. Neither do we have to lose our kids to be "on fire" for God or to be effective in the marketplace. In fact, I think God will use the maturity that is cultivated when we build relationships with those close to us as a platform to dealing more effectively with situations beyond family and friends.

Big things can happen when we do small well.

WHAT'S YOUR AMBITION?

The Bible talks about ambition. Ambition is defined as an eager or strong desire to achieve something. "Make it your ambition to lead a quiet life," the apostle Paul commands members of the early church, "to mind your own business and to work with your hands, just as we told you, so that your daily life may win the respect of outsiders" (1 Thess. 4:11–12). The command is basically, make it your ambition to *stay put and live well*.

Compare this ambition to that of the apostle himself, as a full-time minister: "It has always been my ambition to preach the gospel where Christ was not known" (Rom. 15:20). A big part of Paul's calling demanded that he focus his energies on preaching and teaching the gospel from place to place. But he never projects his personal calling on the individuals in the churches he started. Instead he tells them to lead quiet daily lives.

I get raised eyebrows whenever I say I believe the best way to reach the world is to keep as many people as possible *out* of full-time ministry. But I think it is true. I think ministers have done a disservice to the body of Christ (especially in the evangelical and charismatic traditions) by leaving the impression that the center of God's attention is on the apostles, prophets, evangelists, pastors, and teachers (full-time ministers).

I don't believe that. I don't think God waits from Sunday to Sunday or from service to service, anticipating another opportunity to move on the earth. I think He wants to get into the fabric of our everyday, boring lives. I think He loves our *ordinary zone*. What if the Mark 16:15 mandate to "go into all the world and preach" could be read, "As you go into your everyday world, preach!"?

I'm suggesting that the layperson's biblical strategy for preaching the gospel in her world is very different from a minister's strategy. When you watch Paul and the other preachers in the Bible, it is obvious that God gifted them to garner interest in the gospel message through their preaching and their charismatic presence or ministry. There is a miracle involved in preaching. Preachers create a question in the minds of unbelievers to consider Jesus simply by preaching. Creating the question is at the heart of the Great Commission.

But how does the layperson do it? (Generally people flee by the thousands when laypeople preach.) How does the typical mom with three kids still in diapers reach the world? How does the high-school student, who is trying to discover who she is and where she fits in the world, reach others for Jesus? How does the retired person struggling with health issues or intensely caring for an elderly parent reach the world?

The answer is found in Peter's writing. He says as we live our lives in a way that shows we have "set apart Christ as Lord" in our hearts, we will create a question in the minds of others. Peter contends that the role of the believer is to "always be prepared to give an answer" to the emerging questions from those who observe our lives (1 Peter 3:15).

Somehow, as we "set apart Christ as Lord" in our hearts, we start looking different. We become "marked" with otherworldly bright spots (joy, peace, kindness, patience, hope, etc). These "bright spots" create a question inside of those who are within our sphere of influence. When the question comes, Peter says we are to "answer." I suggest that *answering the question* our lives create *is* lay ministry—it is fulfilling the Great Commission!

DON'T MESS WITH THE ELEPHANTS

Forget about *big*. Abandon the longings for the spectacular. Fall in love with life—the everyday, normal kind. Those who hope for big are usually in a mad dash for significance and destiny. But what they end up with is big ego and a world of fantasy. Most people who talk big don't end up big; they just end up fat in the head—i.e., they turn into fatheads! Most big thinking is not God. And if God really has something big in store for you, you will get to it by doing small actions anyway. Stick with being a believer. Dare to believe that the minor details of your life matter to God. Dare to believe you are not a mistake.

And leave the elephants alone. You'll be happier and healthier if you do.

sour-grace disease: whatever

Grace is an amazing thing. There is no way it makes sense. It is God lovingly chasing us when there is no reason for it. When the psalmist caught a glimpse of the love and favor God had for him, he cried, "This is too much, too wonderful—I can't take it all in!" (Ps. 139:6 MSG).

Neither can we. It may resemble the natural kindness and love that families and married couples share, but it plunges far deeper, and it is way more unconditional and deathless.

Paul prayed that his friends would have the "power to understand, as all God's people should, how wide, how long, how high, and how deep his love really is" (Eph. 3:18 NLT). It takes "power to understand" God's love and grace toward us—God has to help us see it.

I totally get how some think all this is too good to be true. How can it be true? How can God be so reckless about giving to us when we are so good at being so bad? But that is exactly what He is like. We matter to Him, and there is nothing we can do to alter that.

Obviously this begs a question that must be addressed: If God is really like this, what prevents people from taking advantage of His grace?

This popped up in response to Paul's teaching on God's grace in the Bible. Paul claimed that all sin was already dealt with by God's grace—that our sin is no longer an issue. He made securing forgiveness sound so easy and kept it so God-centered that folks started thinking, *If that's the case, why fight sin? Why not just do it? If God responds to sin by giving grace, why not just continue to sin so that grace increases?* (Rom. 6:1, author's paraphrase). Grace became an excuse to continue sinning; people got "sour-grace disease." And they were not the first to be tempted to think this way. Since the beginning, whenever grace has been taught, this thought has always cropped up. But it isn't true.

We can't mess with grace. God designed a true encounter with grace to mess with us. Paul claimed his changed life and his motivation for obeying God was "the grace of God" (1 Cor. 15:10). In another place he wrote that grace "teaches us to say 'No' to ungodliness and worldly passions, and to live self-controlled, upright and godly lives in this present age" (Titus 2:12). Grace messes with *us*.

Grace is a face-to-face encounter with God's love, and when that happens, you end up loving God back. You can't help it any more than I can keep my foot from kicking out when you thump me on that "spot" on my knee. It just happens—it's a reflex. John wrote, "We love because he first loved us" (1 John 4:19). If you have had an authentic revelation of God's love and grace, it will produce love in *you*. It will change you. It is impossible to take advantage of grace, because if you really get it, it *gets you*.

Listen. God may *seem* foolhardy to forgive so easily, to accept and make us belong without caution, but He's no fool—He knows His love ultimately *alters us*. Paul said "the riches of his kindness" (which is the recklessness of His love) always "leads" us to change (Rom. 2:4).

When Jesus spoke to the woman caught in adultery in the gospel of John, He did not condemn her. He told her, "Go, and sin no more" (John 8:11 KJV). He was telling her it was time to *change*. He never said, "Go and sin *some* more." Grace doesn't do that. It isn't something that encourages us to continue sinning without considering consequences. When we encounter the love and grace of God, a transformation occurs that fosters *change*.

Oswald Chambers wrote, "If I receive forgiveness and continue to be bad, I prove that God is immoral in forgiving me, and make a travesty of Redemption. When I accept Jesus Christ's way he transfigures me from within."[1]

We can't help it. Once we are caught by God's love, we are changed, transfigured. However, the change is more fluid than permanent. Too bad.

BACK TO THE SHOWERS

I used to wish God would just change me permanently. When I surveyed my life, there were some areas I was strong in. I have never been tempted to rob banks. (I have a stellar no-robbing-banks commitment.) I have never even considered beating up people, even when they angered me. Arson has never tempted me; neither has alcohol. My behavior has always been impressive in those arenas. And I wanted to be as stable and absolute in my commitment to a consistent devotional life as I was in my "no-arson" commitment, as committed to not stretch the truth or procrastinate or lust as I was to not beat people up.

I wanted God to bite me.

I'd better explain.

Peter Parker, a below-average guy in the Marvel comic series *Spider-Man*, happened to be taking a class where radioactive beams were being tested. In the course of an experiment, a spider crossed the path of a radioactive beam, fell, and landed on Peter's hand, biting him. Peter dizzied, collapsed to the floor, and got up, Spider-Man. The opening song goes: "Spider-Man, Spider-Man, does whatever a spider can."

That's what I wanted God to do. I wanted Him to land on me at the altar and bite my soul in a way that would make me fall down and get back up, Godly Man. I wanted my opening song each day to begin, "Godly Man, Godly Man, does whatever a godly man can." I wanted the transformation to be so deep and so permanent that even if God died, I'd still be godly. Stupid. I know.

But transformation isn't like that. It is much messier. It is a daily (if not minutely) practice of finding the spout where grace comes out. Grace is not native to us; sin is. We have to look beyond ourselves to experience grace. That is the "why" behind the classic spiritual disciplines of prayer, solitude, study, worship, fasting, and so forth. We use those practices to reach out beyond ourselves into the actual, tangible grace of God. It's really there. It's metaphysical but real. When we tap into it, it jacks us up spiritually and trashes the impulses of our lower nature.

We cannot change our own nature, but grace will. The task at hand is to figure out how persons with our unique personalities and mindsets can best tap into grace. For me grace is most easily accessed as I ponder the Scriptures. As I wrestle with texts, grace dawns inside me. My wife, Gail, taps into grace as she sings and worships. Others touch God's grace most by getting together with other believers or by retreating into times of solitude.

The point is, find the spout nearest *you*.

When Paul wrote about grace, he said to not let it be a "vanity" or an ineffective influence in our lives. He said that grace is daily—a "now" thing (2 Cor. 6:2).

Grace is not a yesterday, or a last-week, or a when-I-first-came-to-Jesus experience. It is like the manna God provided the Israelites in the wilderness—it had to be fresh to be eatable. We need fresh "grace bread" to experience the transformation it gives. When we're bad, we need more grace.

I wish grace was a permanent repair, but it's not. It's actually more like a shower. I don't like body odor. If I ever get anywhere

117

near stink, I shower. It might be cool if there was a magic, one-time shower that would forever eliminate all past and future body odor, but there isn't. If you want to remain odor free, you need to have access to a shower—especially if your life is a constant "workout."

Staying sin free and transformed requires frequent "grace showers." In other words, grace demands participation. We need to *work* grace into our lives, which means we must tangle and wrestle with it through the spiritual discipline of seeking God. I'm convinced that the free, available, abundant grace of God is only secured as we *weary* ourselves in pursuit of it. At one point in Scripture, God says, "You have not called upon me . . . you have not wearied yourselves for me" (Isa. 43:22). Grace is free, but it is not secured without personal cost. Paul said grace was huge in his life because he "worked harder" with it than most had (1 Cor. 15:10).

Are you working to ensure grace is not "in vain" as far as you are concerned? Don't wait until you stink to take a shower. Practice an "odor-prevention" strategy. Go into God's presence and ask Him to invade your thinking, your reasoning, and your will. Ask Him to fill you with faithfulness and joy and peace and kindness. Don't walk into your day until you are jammed with spiritual energy, which will leave little room for your lower nature to blossom. Preventive grace is always much sweeter than recovery grace.

WHEN GRACE GOES SOUR

For me, the most stunning aspect of faith is grace. Grace is that unmerited, incautious favor of God that most of us never tire hearing about. There is just something about it—whenever it comes, it changes what *is* into something *grander*. That is what I love about the gospel. It is a message of *grace*, and because of that, wherever it goes, it brings change.

sour-grace disease: whatever

But some groups who call themselves "grace" people make me nervous. I get the feeling that they spell grace g-r-e-a-s-e. They don't talk about grace as something that changes them as much as something that lets them *slide by* with whatever they feel like doing—even sinful things. But grace yields freedom *from* sin, not freedom *to* sin. Justifying sin by appealing to grace sours the grace experience by turning it into something God never intended to be. Grace never says, "Whatever." It always says, "No" to "ungodliness" and "Yes" to "upright and godly" living (Titus 2:12).

I'm convinced that the people who use grace as an excuse to sin aren't experiencing it at all. They may have experienced grace in the past or they may have just heard about it, but they are not experiencing it *now*. You can't experience the grace of God and continue being bad. If you are being bad today, it's because you *are not* experiencing grace today. Grace doesn't promise immunity from sinful consequences; it promises power to live above sin.

It's true that if you miss grace to prevent sin, you can tap into grace that brings the forgiveness of sin. God has a very effective 911 system. But using 911 is not a thing to boast about. And if you use 911 flippantly, you get in trouble. Grace is never a license to sin.

In fact, it is the grace of God that brings judgment for sin. Just as God tells us to discipline our children, and that if we do not discipline them, we, in effect, *hate* them (Prov. 13:24), He disciplines us too—because he loves us. But there are folks in the "grace" crowd that think God *never* does anything quite so negative. He only wants us to be happy, content, always having a good time—even if we are naughty. He is just *soooo* loving.

But I think they might have God confused with Grandpa. Grandpa tends to overlook wrongdoing, and he always avoids confrontation. Grandpa's goal at the end of the day is only that all had a good time. But Jesus didn't tell us to pray, "Our Grandpa in heaven." He said to pray, "Our Father in heaven" (Matt. 6:9).

Scripture is clear. God is our Father, and He "disciplines us for our good, that we may share in his holiness" (Heb. 12:10). God doesn't just love us with a smile while He distributes playful impulses of joy into our souls. He sometimes gets hard with us and treats us in a way that doesn't seem "pleasant at the time, but painful" (v.11). We are His sons and daughters. We are the chosen, His sent ones. He believes in us, He trusts us, and He calls upon us to represent Him. You and I matter. He isn't kidding about destiny. He consistently asks us to be part of His salvation history. We are called to a purpose. The Bible applauds a guy who "served God's purpose in his own generation" (Acts 13:36). That's what He wants all of us to do. That's why we are here.

If we say no to His plan, He will back off. That is a scary enterprise. When Israel said no to God, He said of them, "My people would not listen to me; Israel would not submit to me. So I gave them over to their stubborn hearts to follow their own devices" (Ps. 81:11–12).

I don't want to be left to my "own devices," do *you*?

JUDGMENT

God is not the one who makes life ugly for us. But there are times He backs off and our own ugliness takes over. It's called "judgment." Judgment is not something God *does* to us as much as it is something He *lets happen* to us.

Jesus claimed that the Father doesn't judge people (John 5:22). Judgment exists, but Jesus said it was His "word" that judged people (John 12:48). He talked about "the person who hears my words but does not keep them" (v. 47) and said he would be judged by the very words he spoke—not by the *person* of God. That means God is never out to "get you." But, like any good father, God will eventually no longer protect us from the persistent negative actions that we refuse to renounce. If we don't repent, He lets us experience the harvest of our sin. "Do not be deceived," Paul warns. "God cannot be mocked. A man reaps what he sows. The one who sows to please his sinful nature, from that nature will reap destruction" (Gal. 6:7–8).

The good news is, God usually hangs in there a long, long time, shielding us from our own devices for as long as possible and giving us every chance to turn away from our sinful actions. He does not withdraw His protection from us easily. He knows we are knuckleheads. The psalmist said it best: "He does not treat us as our sins deserve or repay us according to our iniquities . . . for he knows how we are formed; he remembers that we are dust" (Ps. 103:10, 14).

But if we persistently resist Him, He will eventually let us experience our own way. Here is a scary text: "God opposes the proud but gives grace to the humble" (James 4:6). Having God in opposition to us can never be a good thing.

The idea of judgment is simple. God is trying to help us. If we say no to Him, eventually He leaves us alone. That is judgment—God backing out of our lives. It is the result of our refusal to submit to the person of Jesus—to His help and love. When we reject Jesus, we reject God Himself, along with all His freedom and forgiveness. Where freedom and forgiveness are absent, there is judgment. It comes when we refuse God's mercy. The Scripture says, "Did you think that because he's such a nice God, he'd let you off the hook? Better think this one through from the beginning. God is kind, but he's not soft. In kindness he takes us firmly by the hand and leads us into a radical life-change. You're not getting by with anything. Every refusal and avoidance of God adds fuel to the fire. The day is coming when it's going to blaze hot and high, God's fiery and righteous judgment" (Rom. 2:4–6 MSG).

Grace helps us act right and recover from acting wrong. Anyone who would try to take advantage of grace could never get away with it. He may fool people in the church. He may fool parents and close friends, but never God. God "looks at the heart" (1 Sam. 16:7). He knows what's going on. No one can misuse the grace of God.

> The great grace man, the apostle Paul, heralded, "Notice how God is both kind and severe. He is severe to those who disobeyed, but kind to you as you continue to trust in his kindness. But if you stop trusting, you also will be cut off" (Rom. 11:22 NLT).

That said, getting out from under judgment is a simple matter. If you have been heading west for fifty years, but turn to head east, the change is instant—you are now heading east. If you ever come to a place where you think you might be under judgment, don't fear—just turn toward God. Instantly you will abort all judgment and find yourself back in the favor and grace of God. (Remember the prodigal son story?) Why is it so easy? Because what Jesus did on the cross carries much more weight in God's eyes than anything you or I could do or not do, and as a result, the grace of forgiveness is *never* held back from us. As long as you have breath, there is hope for you.

So do you want to be healed of sour-grace disease? Then do a 180. You won't regret it.

14

ecology pathology: trashing the planet

I grew up an earth *user*. Along with millions of other Americans, I shamelessly tossed out my McDonald's remnants on the highways and byways as I traveled along, singing a song. Then I saw the public service announcement with the old American Indian. As he looked at the pollution around America, a tear ran down his cheek. That was a watershed moment for me where my ecological worldview was concerned.

Maybe we shouldn't trash the planet, I thought.

But it didn't last. After I came to Jesus and realized He was going to return sometime in the next couple of months, I began to think, *Why not trash this place? We're out of here soon anyway.* (I know this sounds bad—and it was.) I even found verses to back up my irreverence for the environment. I saw that God Himself was eventually going to trash the planet with fire (2 Peter 3:10), so a few Styrofoam cups shouldn't matter. I figured since the world was destined for doom, who cares if we leave it a mess, or rape it for the natural resources we need, without regard for replacing them?

My anticonservation bias was spiritualized and politicized—I mocked the conservationists. I thought that "they exchanged the truth of God for a lie, and worshiped and served created things rather than the Creator" (Rom. 1:25). They were tree-worshipping heathens to me. Any verses that suggested God cared about the condition of the earth eluded me.

BECOMING STEWARDS

I was in seminary when I first saw what the Bible taught about the sacredness of the environment. One day I caught my Old Testament professor roaming around campus after lunch to collect soda cans from receptacles he had set up. I thought he was doing it for the money, but when I asked him about it, he said, "Actually, I use the money I make for missions, but I want to do what I can to conserve the earth's resources and keep it clean to honor God. Sin has sullied it enough."

I wrinkled my eyebrows in surprise. I had never thought in those terms and told him so. He smiled and told me that God *does* care about the earth, that His care is the only thing that explains *why* he told Adam and Eve to "work and take care of" the earth (Gen. 2:15). It also explains why God told Israel to make sure the land got the rest that was its due (Lev. 25:4). He even judged Israel for *not* giving the land rest.

When I stopped to consider that God created this planet and in Genesis 1:28 invited humanity to participate with Him in sustaining it—to bring His rule into it—the picture changed for me. I saw that God doesn't want us to carelessly trash the planet in the name of progress even if we think Jesus is coming back soon. He wants us to use it responsibly and to care for it.

If this is true, doesn't that mean we need to embrace practices like only cutting down as many trees as we can replace with seedlings? Or never dumping more waste in our water or air than the environment can recover from? In other words, should we not be *stewards* instead of *users* of this planet?

ecologogy pathology: trashing the planet

What if God loves this place? What if conservation glorifies God? What if the followers of Jesus become the champions of environmental issues?

Then we won't have ecology pathology—and we won't trash the planet.

15

pathological do-gooding:
the martha syndrome

When was the last time you got a pat on the back for taking it easy? We don't dole out awards for those who get adequate rest. We only applaud overachievers. We shun the undercommitted. Our culture adores those who work seventy to eighty hours a week moving and shaking the world. If you are willing to overextend yourself, you have a shot at winning the race of the rats.

But at what cost?

Jesus said, "What good is it for a man to gain the whole world, yet forfeit his soul?" (Mark 8:36). If you lose your soul—your peace, your joy, your sense of inner tone—in the pursuit of something, it's never worth it. But our culture doesn't agree. We have produced a nation of driven people. And we are trying to conquer the whole world by the weekend. Driven people are not necessarily bad people. They do good things. They start organizations, employ lots of people, and benefit the world greatly. But the cost to them on a personal level is often staggering—they lose their own souls.

Certainly God has called us to "do-gooding." But *doing* good things and being *driven* to do good things are two completely different things. Driven people only know the concept of "more." Always more—*more* achievement, *more* effectiveness, *more* accomplishment, which they believe will yield *more* personal satisfaction and *more* acceptance by others. But usually the exact opposite occurs. They may achieve success but never experience fulfillment, and rabid achievers usually drive people away.

THE MARTHA SYNDROME

There is a story in the Gospels that gives us a snapshot of a do-gooder named Martha. Jesus and His disciples had gone to this woman's house for lunch. The Bible says Martha was "distracted by all the preparations that had to be made" (Luke 10:40). Her sister, Mary, on the other hand, was just enjoying Jesus and the other guests. When Martha feels she isn't getting close enough to perfect, she tries to solicit the help of Mary.

Martha interrupts the conversation Mary is having with Jesus and says to Him, "Lord, don't you care that my sister has left me to do the work by myself? Tell her to help me!"

Jesus responds, "You are worried and upset about many things, but only one thing is needed" (Luke 10:38–40).

"Worried and upset about many things" pretty much sums up the life of a person who is committed to do-gooding. In fact, left unchecked, it blossoms into full-vented perfectionism, which is do-gooding gone pathological. But what if "perfect" is not what God is after from our lives?

Jesus told Martha to chill out. From the context you get the picture that Martha was preparing a huge meal and wanted to make everything just right for Jesus. And you can understand why. But Jesus told her that not everything had to be perfect at that lunch—it was just lunch. He said only "one thing" was needed—perhaps some tuna-fish sandwiches or PB&Js, certainly not a huge gourmet, multicourse meal. He wanted Martha to relax and spend some time with Him. He wanted her to see that He valued human beings more than what human beings *do*.

I don't think God is looking for perfect moms or perfect dads or perfect wives or perfect husbands or perfect citizens or perfect churchgoers—or perfect *anything*. In fact, one could argue on biblical grounds that we can never pull off "perfect," anyway—no matter how hard we try. It seems that what God is after is much more relational than do-gooding affords.

But perfectionists lurk everywhere in our culture—especially in the church. These boys and girls believe there are standards that must be hit consistently if they are ever going to feel good about themselves. But they set the bar so impossibly high that it yields a fear of failure that causes them to be driven—even compulsive. Competitiveness, aggressiveness, and even manipulation dawns when people try to succeed at any cost. This crowd definitely loses perspective.

A PERFORMANCE-BASED WORLD

Though God did not originally design it this way, we live in a performance-based world. It doesn't take us long to figure out that we get further with mom and dad if we *obey* and *comply*; that our siblings are nicer if we *act* the way they want us to; and that colonies of friends will buzz for our attention if we *perform* admirably. Teachers' pets are chosen based on achievement. Bosses choose favorites based on their accomplishments; and religious leaders favor the "spiritual" ones who participate in everything the leaders concoct. So, from parents to siblings to friends to . . . we have had the "perform-to-belong" belief reinforced again and again. It's easy to believe this dysfunction is normal and to assume God thinks this way too.

We often put our experience-based perceptions off on God. So we assume He loves us based on how we act—that's how everybody else loves us. Accepting this belief pushes us in a race for the top. We try to outshine, outlook, and outdo those around us. We feel the need to call attention to our gifts, intelligence, talent, possessions, beauty—anything that might make us look good, while covering up what isn't beautifying about us. If this isn't right, it sure is the way things are.

Though performance impresses people, it doesn't impress God. God's love for us has nothing to do with what we do. This means God isn't looking for something inside us to merit His love or to find encouragement to love us. He knows we don't have much going for ourselves. He knows that, ever since the tragic Fall in Genesis 3, every person born is a kind of born loser. The apostle Paul wrote concerning the human race, "No one is good—not even one" (Rom. 3:10 NLT) and that all have "sinned" and "fall short" of what God intended (v. 23). Each of us is deeply flawed because of sin. C. S. Lewis wrote concerning the nature of man, "Look for yourself and you will find in the long run only hatred, loneliness, despair, rage, ruin and decay."[1] Not a pretty picture.

But God looks past all the bad in us and places value on us. Scripture claims that He did this "while we were still sinners" (Rom. 5:8). Our performance should have made God run *from* us, but He ran *to* us. An understanding of this kind of love bashes the idea that performance is the basis for being accepted and belonging. We can come *just as we are*.

To suggest that God expresses love toward you and me because of some way we act offends Him (Rom. 11:35). We do not initiate this. God is the one who initiates love for us. His love is not a response; it's the way He is. God is love (1 John 4:8). If we let that touch us, we will taste the security of always being loved no matter what!

PERFECTIONISM LEADS TO COMPARISONS

When I first decided to make my life matter for God, I kept bumping into people who seemed to delight in making my experiences appear less than theirs. I prayed, but it never seemed to be as effective as the prayers of others—or so they said. I read my Bible, but I got the feeling I didn't do it as much as anyone else or with the deep understanding they had. Everything I did seemed to fall short compared to those around me.

I remember going around, baring my soul about how I wrestled with sin, and how my attitudes stunk, and how my commitment to Christ was less-than-stellar. Some folks would take it all in, pop a Bible verse at me, and tell me to go to the altar to let God continue to change me. Good advice, but they left me with the impression that no one else had problems like I did. The sense I got was that if I kept growing, I could someday *be like them*—holy and *problem free.*

Though the Bible repeatedly encourages us to "set an example" for others to follow (1 Tim. 4:12), and though we are to "spur one another on toward love and good deeds" (Heb. 10:24), there is a huge difference between living an exemplary life that encourages others to do better and creating a better-than-thou environment, where destructive comparisons take place.

Paul warns that comparing yourself with other people is "not wise" (2 Cor. 10:12). Why not? Because comparison breeds a potpourri of negatives—from competition and envy to condemnation and unhealthy one-upping. A person's sense of identity gets destroyed in these kinds of environments. But often we stick around even when things are unhealthy. I think we do because we all long to belong.

The sad thing is, many church cultures and leadership paradigms are driven by comparison and competition for perfection. And there are wagonloads of condemnation (both silent and vocal) for those who can't reach the bar. It doesn't take long for churches like these to eviscerate the personhood of a member who is struggling to *fit in.* When that happens, people begin to feel inadequate and they burn out trying to follow unrealistic lists of things they feel they *should* do or *could* do. Christianity starts to get hard for them—no "abundant life" about it. And, as far as God's unconditional love is concerned? It seems like a fairy tale for them—though it might be true for others who perform better.

WHY WE'RE SUSCEPTIBLE

I get a disconcerted ache in my soul pretty often. Sometimes I respond by eating some candy or a piece of cake. I'm not really hungry, just achy. Sometimes I run to the store to buy something fun when I feel that icky soul twinge arising. I don't really need anything. I'm just unsettled, and buying a new thing seems to make the unsettled ache a little more bearable, or at least ignorable. There are even times when my achy, breaky heart pushes me down inappropriate trails of worry, lust, or envy—all the negative, soul-bruising stuff. This is when I thank God for his "911" ministry of deliverance and forgiveness, and friends of grace who cover us with love and accountability. The less time spent down those trails, the better.

I think the capacity to "ache" in the human soul is really a gift from God to nudge us toward Jesus. The Scripture encourages us to interpret all the aches within our heart as "highways" back to God (Ps. 84:5 NASB).

The psalmist got it right. He said he had to seek God because earth is a "dry and weary land where there is no water" (Ps. 63:1). He interpreted his soul ache as a "thirst" and "longing" for God. When we fail to do that, we are off to the fridge, the mall, or the land of inappropriate longings.

Though I know this, there is one area where I get stumped more often than I care to admit. It's the area of being a do-gooder. Don't misunderstand me; it's good to do good things and to do them well. But like anything else, too much of a good thing is no longer a good thing. Often when my own soul ache arises (that inner, unsettling sense that we all get), I default to doing things to make myself feel better about me. My life becomes a study in to-dos. And I am hooked on the feeling that comes when I check off one of my to-dos. Getting things into the "Done" column is a high for me. Consequently, when my soul aches, instead of running to my secret closet to call home to my God and drink of the eternal water that really satisfies, I think, *I've gotta get some more stuff done.* I'm no longer a human *being.* I am a human *doing.* And my life turns to "do-do."

Jesus talked about folks who did all kinds of good works but said they were really "evildoers" (Matt. 7:23). Why? Because they were doing good things with a wrong motive. And that, my friend, is the rub. *Why* do you do good works? Are you performing for a prize? Are you trying to garner acceptance from a particular group? To make up for past failure (penance)? To earn a position? Are you trying to cover up boredom or discontentment? Or maybe to prove your worth to God, yourself, or others? What are you trying to do?

Motive is a huge thing with God. Doing good deeds with a wrong motive nullifies the goodness of the work done. Paul claimed that works are either made of "wood, hay, [and] straw"—things easily destroyed, or of "gold, silver, [and] costly stones"—things that endure (1 Cor. 3:12). And it all has to do with the motive behind why deeds are done. Motive is everything.

The only legitimate motive for good works is the power of grace in the human heart. Paul said, "By the grace of God I am what I am" (1 Cor. 15:10). He also said we become "eager to do what is good" because of God's grace (Titus 2:14). God's favor in our lives enters the human soul, and the soul has a reflex—a reflex that is just as sure as the blinking reflex of the human eye. Take a jab close to the human eye and try *not* to blink. You can't. The eye must blink. It's an autonomic reflex. The soul's reflex to grace is the doing of good works. Without premeditated thought, we start to love. We start to act *for* others. We act for the good of the kingdom of God.

We can't help ourselves—we bear fruit. It is the natural reflex of the soul to grace.

This is not doing good to be accepted. It is not doing good to fill our own need for significance or self-actualization. This is not "pathological do-gooding." This is God causing us to bring forth. It is living to the full.

The doing of good deeds is important as believers—but not as a performance in order to belong. We do good deeds *because* we belong.

The core of the disease I call pathological do-gooding is a belief that performance is the key to acceptance. That is a lie. However, only God can erase that deception by flooding us with His unconditional love through the person Jesus Christ. It is His unconditional love that gives us an unshakable feeling of worth and a deep sense of significance. These were the gifts granted because we are His creations.

We don't act to *become*. We *are* what we *are* by His grace; therefore we *act*. Understanding these thoughts is the cure for pathological do-gooding.

16

spiritual blindness:
looking beyond the seen

I'm living my whole life for someone I've never seen—kind of weird when you think about it. But that's the way faith works. God is invisible, though we see hints of His activity all around us. Faith is more of a Goldilocks experience than anything else. The bears only knew that someone had been eating their porridge, sitting in their chairs, and lying on their beds. It wasn't till the end of the story that they run into that *someone*: Goldilocks. We don't get to see God till the end either.

According to Paul, Satan has "blinded the minds" of people against God (2 Cor. 4:4). I think he can pull that off so easily precisely because God *is* invisible. Satan causes us to miss the clues God leaves. Jesus said the Father "causes [the] sun to rise" and "sends rain" (Matt. 5:45). We chalk it up to nature. Jesus said we only think about God because we are "taught by God" to do so (John 6:45). But anthropologists tell us belief in God is a human concoction. We get blinded.

Biblically, one of the main reasons we pray is to improve our spiritual *sight*. Paul told people he was praying that God would open the "eyes" of their hearts so they could know God better and be able to see His plans and acts in their lives. We need divine intervention to "catch" God. And once sight comes, we are urged to stay focused on "what is unseen" (2 Cor. 4:18). How odd. How do you live focused on what you don't see? It would be like steering your car with your eyes shut, while looking inside. Sounds like Luke Skywalker, Jedi, *listen-to-the-force* stuff. However, if we can pull it off, our lives become different.

YOU ARE WHAT YOU SEE

I was in the Milwaukee airport when I spotted them; the couple had to be in their seventies. The fact that they looked so much alike is what struck me. They were not alike in a blood-relative way; it was a different way. Their facial expressions, their voice inflections and hand motions, their eyes—the resemblance was notable. They were husband and wife. Marriage partners start looking and sounding like one another after a while, at least the ones in love do. But this couple took "look alike" to a whole new level. Their likenesses were an obvious result of lots of gazing time. And at seventy their care for each other was unmistakable. *Pretty cool,* I thought as I kept staring at them (through my fingers, of course).

We end up looking like the things we focus on. The writer of Hebrews tells us to "fix our eyes on Jesus" (12:2). Why? When we look at Jesus, we become like Him. John wrote, "We know that when he appears, we shall be like him, for we shall see him as he is" (1 John 3:2). To *see Him* is to become like Him. It's a kind of law of *attention.*

That's why the psalmist asked God to help him turn his eyes from "worthless things" (Ps. 119:37). He didn't want to become "worthless." The old Sunday school song goes, "Be careful little eyes, what you see." Jesus talked about people who end up with "bad eyes." He said their whole lives end up "full of darkness" (Matt. 6:22–23). Bad eyes are eyes that are on the wrong things. What we attend to is important.

Where we look is where we end up going, which poses a provocative question: What if transformation is more about *where* we fix our

135

eyes (our attention) and less about using our super willpower to force ourselves to be different?

PAY ATTENTION TO YOUR ATTENTION

Jesus said, "For where your treasure is, there will your heart be also" (Matt. 6:21). He is basically saying, "Whatever you pay attention to, that is where your heart will be—and that is what you will find yourself desiring." This is a radical concept if you think about it.

All of us have times when we desire things that were "forbidden" in God's Word. All God-lovers hate doing that. When I was a new believer, I often wept at the altars of our little country church, asking God to permanently change my heart so I wouldn't stray into the forbidden. I made commitments. I promised. I made covenants. I tried everything I could, only to go out and mess up again and again.

At the time, I thought the reason I was paying attention to the wrong things was because my heart was evil and was pushing me toward evil. If I had a bent toward sin, I was sure my heart was in a wrong place and I needed some kind of spiritual "heart surgery." It didn't dawn on me until I saw this verse in Matthew years later, that our attention doesn't follow our hearts as much as our hearts follow our attention. Jesus said that whatever you "treasure"—what has your attention—that is where your heart will be.

This means our "forbidden" desires don't launch from the heart. We desire wrong things because we get focused on and pay attention to wrong things. We have focus problems, not heart ones! Jesus did *not* say, "Whatever you have a desire for is what you will pay attention to." He said the exact opposite. He showed us that our *desire* (heart) follows our attention (or what we have been focusing on).

Here is a good example. You go for months without even thinking about purchasing a new car. Then you happen upon a new car lot, and something amazing transpires. You step into the showroom and walk up to one of the shiny new vehicles. You sit in the driver's seat, shut the door, and that new-car aroma fills your nostrils. Your hands grip the steering wheel, and your heart begins to race at the thought of owning a wonder machine like this one. Suddenly, leaping from within you comes this *desire*—this deep, heartfelt longing to *buy this car.* You are sure it must be the Lord. It came right out of your heart. You think, *Who cares if I can't afford it? Didn't God promise to give me the desires of my heart? Besides, He will provide!*

But don't be fooled. Your heart follows your focus. Whatever you attend to captures and catapults desire—and the more you attend to it, the stronger the desire. As goes your attention, so goes your heart. When you find yourself desiring wrong things, don't assume your *heart* led you astray; your focus did. That is why the nature of temptation is the way it is. In temptation, Satan tries to get our attention as completely as possible. If he can get our *attention,* he has a shot at polluting our hearts.

Did you ever wonder why the God of the Bible is a God of the miraculous? Miracles make people turn their heads; it gets their attention. If God can get people's *attention,* He has a shot at their hearts.

It helped me when I realized that my heart wasn't the root of all wrong desire, but that wrong desires stemmed from my misplaced interest. Then I realized I needed to be more careful about managing my attention. Now, when wrong desire dawns in me, though I know I need a touch from God to correct my heart, I also realize that I need to work on my focus. Right focus is what keeps a right heart. It's the path to consistent freedom. The book of Hebrews teaches, "We must pay more careful attention, therefore, to what we have heard, so that we do not drift away" (2:1).

SPIRITUAL PERISCOPES

The old prophet was in the middle of a miracle when he paused and prayed concerning his servant, "O LORD, open his eyes so he may see" (2 Kings 6:17). God did, and the prophet's servant "caught" what he had been missing—God's action all around him. We always need help from the Divine to catch divine action, because God works from the unseen to the seen. And often when the "seen" shows up, we're not exactly sure how it got there—maybe God, maybe coincidence.

I think God's primary way of helping us "see" Him is through our participation in the classic disciplines of Christianity. Stuff like prayer, study, silence, etc. Sadly, many have used these things wrongly, as religious performance. But they were designed by God to help us *see* into another dimension, the spiritual one.

When I was a kid, we used to play with toy periscopes in our army or spy games. They were great. We could peek around corners or over fences taller than us. We got perspectives we couldn't have had with the naked eye. Prayer is a kind of periscope. It gives us perspective that we can't get with the naked eye. We start to see things we would have never been able to see before.

Study is a periscope too. I love to pray the Scriptures. I see things that, up to that moment, I was missing. Just this morning I woke up, still tired and a little blurred spiritually, and thought, *God must be on vacation.* But I've been at this for a while and know some tricks of the trade. I got out my spiritual periscope of praying promises and went after it.

> *You are all around me, my Father in the heavens.* (Matt. 6:9)
>
> *For some reason, You are thinking of me right now.* (Ps. 139:18)
>
> *You think I am worth Jesus—that I matter.* (Rom. 5:8)
>
> *You are at work in me right now, causing me to want to do Your will and giving me the power to do it.* (Phil. 2:13)

138

You knew this day was coming before it got here, and You have already thought through what I need. (Matt. 6:11, 2 Peter 1:3)

Thank You for being with me today. (Heb. 13:5–6)

Fill me with Your Holy Spirit as I wait in silence and yield my mind and emotions to you. (Eph. 5:18; Gal. 5:22–23)

As I rehearsed these Bible-based prayers, God's presence began to manifest. Peace came. Confidence arose. *It's You, Lord, that I'm after in life,* I thought. This is about God, not about what I do. And I thought, *I want to trust You today; I want to obey You today.* Then I began thinking through my to-dos and plan while reflecting on the Presence for any "veto" or special guidance (though I rarely get it).

Spiritual periscopes make faith "otherly." They help us see beyond ourselves to the presence of a real Person, God. They help us remember that He is in the audience of our lives—the most important One in the audience.

AN AUDIENCE OF ONE

"In that day men will look to their Maker and turn their eyes to the Holy One of Israel" (Isa. 17:7).

When I was in college, I was part of a very cheesy swing choir. It was the '70s, and we were doing "Up with People." My new girl-friend, Gail (now my bride), was in the audience. The whole time I was performing in front of the audience of hundreds, I was really only performing for *one*—Gail. I knew where she was sitting. I kept glancing over at her. I did my best that night, for her. She was my audience of *one*.

For those of us who apprentice with Jesus, everything we do is to be done to an audience of One. Paul commands us to work, play, rest, worship, eat, sleep, *whatever*, directly for God and "to him"

139

(Rom. 11:36). Paul said we should work "with an eye to obeying the real Master, Christ" (Eph. 6:5 MSG). Our audience is God.

This is really reverence for God, although *reverence* is a word that is a little hazy to us. Basically, the person you are reverencing *sticks out*—you can't get him or her off your mind. And reverence can yield both positive and negative results.

Imagine meeting a famous person like Billy Graham. When with him, he would stick out so profoundly that you may find it hard to put an intelligent sentence together. You may become so self-critical that you battle internally about what to do with your hands. Those are examples of a negative result of reverence. The Bible says overreverence for people brings "a snare" (Prov. 29:25). It can be paralyzing.

But reverencing God produces positive results. Scripture says reverence for God brings "a future hope for you, and your hope will not be cut off" (Prov. 23:18). We are instructed to cultivate a reverence for God—to let him *stick out* to us more than others do. This is true even in the presence of the important people of our lives, like our supervisors. Paul said, "And work with a smile on your face, always keeping in mind that no matter who happens to be giving the orders, you're really serving God" (Eph. 6:7 MSG).

If we make our audience other people and not God, we open Pandora's box. "Am I now trying to win the approval of men, or of God? Or am I trying to please men? If I were still trying to please men, I would not be a servant of Christ" (Gal. 1:10). The greatest reverence should go to God, not people. The psalmist was committed to practicing God's *stick-out* presence. He said, "I have set the LORD always before me" (Ps. 16:8).

MAKING GOD HAPPY

The writer of Hebrews wrote, "It's impossible to please God apart from faith. And why? Because anyone who wants to approach God must believe both that he exists and that he cares enough to respond to those who seek him" (11:6 MSG).

Spiritual blindness makes us ignore God. It makes Him irrelevant. If God is deemed irrelevant, we won't "seek him" and we won't have faith. There is nothing pleasing to God about that. But spiritual blindness can lift, and when it does, it changes everything.

Paul said that he constantly prayed for blindness to be lifted from those he loved (Eph. 1:17). We should do the same. We need to pray for people everywhere so they can "catch" God—so they won't miss His clues. When faith dawns in people, God is pleased! Often when I am at the mall or at an airport or just driving along, I look at people and send out "arrow prayers." Those are short, one-sentence prayers asking God to open their eyes to what He is doing in their lives, to remove their spiritual blindness. Many people have *never* been prayed for. Ultimately, I think the prayers of the saints mean eternal life or death for folks. We need to pray.

So pray!

17

reverse hypochondria: the gift of pain

I really want to live right. I want to love and be loved. I want to like and be liked. I want to be transparent, giving, selfless, kind, gentle, full of the fruit of the Holy Spirit—the whole deal. And I have my moments. After times of abandon in His presence in prayer, study, meditation, or reflection, I carry a fragrance, a palpable weight that steadies my soul and makes me bigger than I am.

But the reality is, when the glory of devotion begins to fade and I enter the rough-and-tumble of my day, I find deep within myself a piece that is part fraud and poisoned with deceit. Something in me still loves selfishness and wants to maneuver things to my own advantage. I don't like that self-centeredness is there, and I love to pretend that it isn't.

I think this applies to all of us. If we were really honest with ourselves, we would have to admit that on some level we are always less than we should be. There is always something yucky lurking. Something despairing. To think that there is a corrupted part of us that will never be fixed till we leave this planet is kind of a depressing thought.

Hypochondriacs always think they are sick. On a spiritual plane, most are reverse hypochondriacs. We don't think we are sick; we always think we are well, even when we're not. And that can kill us.

All those who have gone before us, believers throughout history, understand that we should be afraid of ourselves. Yes, we have our bright spots, but there is a worm in the apple of the human condition. Every one of us is capable of bad things. We are all from the land of broken toys.

One of the reasons Vietnam vets struggle so is because they did things when immersed in the madness of war that they never imagined they could do. We must face the fact that, given the right set of circumstances, we are capable of anything. Each of us needs to realize that, but for the grace of God, there go I. I believe there is *no* sin that we would not commit, no perverse act in which we would not participate, if the conditions were right. We should be afraid of ourselves.

ZEROS WITHOUT GOD

All believers who ever stood out in history progressed in their relationship with the Lord with a combination of a deep sense of their own sinfulness and a profound appreciation of what God accomplished in them through their faith in Jesus Christ. People like Brother Lawrence, Teresa of Avila, Martin Luther, John Calvin, Madame Guyon, John Wesley, Francis Schaeffer, and a host of others, were not afraid to talk about their sinful bent and would even boast of their weaknesses, while claiming that their brokenness helped them experience the life available in Jesus.

If you feel like a bit of a loser because you are always falling short of doing the things you *should*—if your life is south of stellar—you're actually in a better place than you may realize. God likes people who aren't real impressed with themselves.

Just look at the kind of people God has recruited for His work throughout history. When He called Moses, Moses protested, saying he wasn't "eloquent" and was actually "slow of speech and tongue." Then he whined, "O Lord, please send someone else to do it" (Ex. 4:10, 13).

Gideon didn't think very highly of himself. He told God he was from the "weakest" family in town and that he was the "least" of that weak clan (Judges 6:15). Jeremiah moaned that he didn't know "how to speak" because he was "only a child" (Jer. 1:6). Jesus' own disciples weren't part of the *Who's Who* crowd. They were not the scholars, the philosophers, the politicians, or the power brokers of the day. They were just fishermen and tax collectors—common folk.

But it seems God likes it that way.

Once while praying, Jesus was praising God for hiding spiritual reality from "the wise and learned" (Luke 10:21). God *hides* things from folks who think they're smart, who seem to have it all together. He doesn't reveal himself to those congested with selfdom.

Instead, He focuses His kingdom on folks who are looking for help beyond themselves—those who have a sense of being broken. That is why the people who experience God are usually those who have been rejected, disenfranchised, hurt, or victimized. Jesus said, "It is not the healthy who need a doctor, but the sick" (Mark 2:17). He said He came for the sick.

This is how Christianity got the reputation of being a "crutch" for weak people. It isn't that faith is an exclusive club for feeble souls; it's that people well-worn by life often feel shattered inside and are usually most open to God's help. Paul surveyed the kind of people that God "called out" to be His Church and said that, of the whole bunch, "not many were wise," "not many were influential," and "not many were of noble birth" (1 Cor. 1:26). In fact, he said most of them were a tad "foolish," "weak," "lowly," and "despised" (vv. 27–28).

It isn't that God ignores those who are of "reputation" in this world; He loves and cares for them. It's that the unwise, insignificant, unrefined, foolish, weak, lowly, despised kind of people are most open to loving and caring back. If you are not dazzled or electrified by yourself—you are not far from the kingdom of God!

I'm not applauding those who belittle themselves; I'm simply saying that people who are super and not in need of others have to discover their depravity before they will be open to being "saved." To be receptive to salvation, you must be willing to admit that you need help—pride precludes that possibility for many who are excessively self-confident.

I *do* think God wants us to genuinely like ourselves, but He does not want us to be self-worshippers. He simply wants our trust to be in Him, not in ourselves. Adam and Eve, in their sinless state of perfection in the Garden of Eden, were called to trust in God even while they were perfect. How much more should we, now that we are on the other side of perfect?

QUIT SUBSCRIBING TO THE LIE

Remember that the lie at the heart of the Fall was that human beings could make it without God—that if they tried hard enough, they could be perfect. Our enemy, Satan, wants us to believe that lie too, that we can all be better—even perfect—if we just try hard enough, long enough, and consistently enough.

But if you have ever set out on a path of spiritual self-improvement, you soon discovered that something was very wrong. You can make all the vows and promises you want, but you will break them sooner or later and become frustrated. No matter how hard you try to stir up your willpower, eventually your will goes AWOL and you end up in sin. Why? Watchmen Nee cites the reason: "Lord I see it now! not only what I have done is wrong, I am wrong!"

I remember how excited I was after I came to Jesus. I wanted to please Him in every way. I was eager to learn all I could about how to walk with God. I quickly began discovering my "responsibilities" in God. He wanted me to pray, witness, study, go to church . . . and at first, I could keep up with it. But the commands kept coming and the expectations kept rising.

Soon I found I couldn't keep all the plates spinning, and I started to break things. I panicked. I tried to cover up my failure by promising to do better. I didn't believe the Christian life was supernatural —beyond human ability. I thought I should be able to get the Christian life down pat, if I just tried a little harder—if I just became more committed. But no matter what I did, I kept crashing.

BEYOND REPAIR

Paul makes a bold statement about himself in the Bible. He says, "What a wretched man I am!" (Rom. 7:24). He was talking about the whole dilemma of wanting to do right but always ending up doing wrong (a concept I understood all too well). His conclusion amazed me. He was comfortable with the revelation that he was a wretch and there was nothing he could do about it on his own.

That completely contradicted everything in me. I didn't want to admit I was a wretch. I wanted to prove to God that I could amount to something.

Paul says another shocking thing. He claims that much of what he has tried to do on his own in order to please God—things that made him look like a go-getter and a good guy—were all *dung*—manure (Phil. 3:8). Without Jesus at the center, as the source of his actions, he regarded himself as a wretch and the content of his life as manure!

Actually, his statements help us catch the secret to the way goodness finds a footing in the believer. Paul refused to pursue perfection through self-effort; he was pursuing the person of Jesus Christ—the perfect One. The secret? *With Jesus, we do well. By ourselves, we do much less than well—we are cesspools.* Paul discovered that humans don't *have* problems; they *are* the problem. He cries rhetorically, "Who will rescue me from this body of death?" (Rom. 7:24). Then he declares, "Jesus Christ our Lord!" (v. 25).

Modern psychology repudiates the whole concept that people are bad, because its supporters have witnessed how debilitating and destructive unresolved guilt is to our lives. In an attempt to reduce feelings of guilt, they try to tell people there is no such thing as right and wrong—no such thing as *sin.* Right and wrong can only be determined on an individual basis. They urge folks to feel only "warm fuzzies" about themselves, to center on their good traits and learn to embrace and even welcome the bad about themselves. They tout artless platitudes like, "I'm OK, you're OK," in an attempt to trivialize the intensity of guilt that people feel.

What modern psychology fails to recognize is that guilt, like physical pain, is actually a gift from God! Can you imagine if you could not feel pain? You'd lean over on a kitchen knife and be oblivious to a cut that could ultimately lead to your bleeding to death. Pain protects us and guards us in life. The capacity for guilt was given to us for the same reason.

Paul tells us that God's Law was given so "everyone in the world may realize guilt before God" (Rom. 3:19 NOR). The "realization" of guilt becomes a kind of "school teacher" for us, leading us to Christ (Gal. 3:24). God never intended for guilt to go unresolved. Its resolve is found in the blood of Jesus. He intended for guilt to motivate us to come to Jesus—not to be an end in itself.

So much energy is wasted as Christians try to find ways to feel better about themselves through self-effort. Because we think God wants us to perform for Him, we often run to the altar, asking God to repair us so we can live more perfect and appropriate lives. "Make me more like Jesus," we cry. But this is a failure to recognize that the Fall caused us to be broken.

Our human pride does not like to accept our wretchedness and dung-manufacturing capacities. We hate to admit that the reason we struggle with feeling good about ourselves is because we are not *supposed* to feel good about ourselves. It is hard to admit that we don't just have negative self-esteem; we have negative *selves*. As the comic-strip character Pogo so aptly put it, "We have met the enemy, and it is us." If we can grasp this, we will understand the need for a continual cultivation of desperation for God. Paul Tournier wrote, "Those who are the most pessimistic about man are the most optimistic about God."[2]

I love this about God. He isn't looking for great performers or people on top of the world, with great faith. He is looking for people who know they are stuck, people who know they can't make it. No way. We are too lost. Too broken. Too inept.

Accepting this truth will actually push us into a place of hope. Once we despair over ourselves, we are ripe to hope entirely in Jesus Christ. Paul wrote, "But [the Lord] said to me, 'My grace is sufficient for you, for my power is made perfect in weakness.' Therefore I will boast all the more gladly about my weaknesses, so that Christ's power may rest on me" (2 Cor. 12:9).

Paul's recognized weakness became the fulcrum for his heart to trust in a power beyond himself. We must accept that more prayer or study or discipline will not fill in all the weak spots we carry, unless the prayer, study, and discipline are methods we are embracing to throw ourselves more wholly upon God. We cannot be strong for God—we can only be strong *with* God.

The truth is, none of us should be surprised at our capacity to be less than we should be. And we should abandon all hope of ever being "fixed" through some magic spiritual moment. We will never graduate from needing Jesus. When we witness our own weakness, we should simply smile at heaven and say, "Lord, this is the best I can do apart from You, and I will continue to be *less*—apart from Your direct working in my life. Let Your power rest on me!"

Our own willpower will *never* be strong enough to make us live right. When we finally abandon the false hope of being able to "get right" and we are filled with despair about our own ability, we will be ready for the change that only comes by God's hand. Buying into our own depravity brings despair—but it is a *good* despair. Knowing we are sick motivates us to keep making appointments with the Great Physician.

18

spiritual amnesia: who's who

I have prayed with enough people at church altars to know that things are good the moment a person crosses the threshold of faith. There is always a burgeoning sensation of joy and peace, a sense of belonging and spiritual ecstasy that lingers for a season. But just as a head injury can cause a person to experience amnesia, the hammer of daily life can cause new believers to forget the wholeness and completeness they once enjoyed. They contract a kind of *spiritual amnesia*.

The writer of the book of Hebrews tells us we should "pay more careful attention . . . to what we have heard, so that we do not drift away" (Heb. 2:1). The phrase "drift away" is a nautical one used to describe how a ship floats off course. Pilots of ships know that drifting off course is what *always* happens. They are constantly aware of it, and it is their job to stay on course. I'm suggesting that "staying on course" spiritually is the job of each believer. We need to be completely aware of the fact that drifting off course is a certainty. Our job as fully devoted followers of Jesus is to fight to stay on course. As a pilotless ship is destined for destruction, we will end up shipwrecked in our faith if we do not stay attentive at the helm.

I think two things we should "pay more careful attention" to are: who God is, and who we are because of God's involvement in our lives.

WHO GOD IS

Who is God? Huge question. We could talk much longer about what we don't know about Him than what we do know. He is all wrapped up in mystery and wonder. Paul said, "Oh, what a wonderful God we have! How great are his riches and wisdom and knowledge! How impossible it is for us to understand his decisions and his methods!" (Rom. 11:33 NLT). Then he said, "Is there anyone around who can explain God?" (Rom. 11:34 MSG).

However, there are a few things we know that are worth keeping constantly in mind. Let's look at three.

1. *He is the One who started the relationship we have with Him.* It certainly *feels* as though we are the ones who discovered God in our lives, but the truth of the matter is, God has always been the One pursuing us. Jesus said, "People can't come to me unless the Father who sent me draws them to me." Faith only makes sense to us because God Himself *made* it make sense. Faith is a gift (Eph. 2:8), and not everyone has it (2 Thess. 3:2). That's why some think having faith is a joke.

Think often of this: *God initiated my faith.* Ponder it. Remember it. Christianity was *never* your responsibility; it was *always* your response to a pursuing God.

2. *This is His story.* In the Christian tradition, human beings are not accidents.

Each person is a dream of God, come true; a destiny; a planned, on-purpose being that God placed in the world as a unique character in His unfolding story. Scripture claims that God "determined the times" in which we would be born and planned "the exact places" we would live (Acts 17:26). The psalmist declared, "All the days ordained for me were written in your book before one of them came to be" (Ps. 139:16).

This means that each one of us matters, and how we fit in this world makes a difference. This isn't a land for the "survival of the fittest"—it is a world for the predestined. But instead of looking for God's predestined plan, many think they are making up their own story. Not so with the ancients, those saints who went before us. Most of them thought, not of making their own story, but of finding their place in the story being told by someone else—God. They believed in the "principle of plenitude." *Plenitude* means "fullness," so they believed creation was *full* of God's ideas and that He had a purpose—and a place—for everything and everyone. Nothing was purely accidental or humanly contrived. The biblical mind-set holds that each of us is born into God's world of plenitude—the world is *His* stage, and we are participants in *His* play. The psalmist said, "Know that the LORD is God. It is he who made us, and we are his" (Ps. 100:3). Those who have gone before us believed success and fulfillment were *not* the results of personal initiative or finding your way as an individual, but in finding the place predestined for you by God.

Just the other night, Gail and I went to a play featuring our beautiful daughter-in-law, Erin. She had one of the lead roles. After the show, we showered her with kudos and asked her how she felt the performance went. She talked mainly about how she felt she did with *her* role. There was no complaining about the others onstage, no talk about wishing she had the lines they had, no attempt on her part to take over another's role, and no discussion about how she wished she could rewrite the script or direct the show differently. She just measured her success by how well she did the job *assigned* to her.

This is how we should hit the stage of life. We should refuse to try to write, produce, direct, or choose the part we want to perform in our own play. We need to see God as the writer, producer, and director. Our ambition should be to *discover* the role God destined us to have, with one thought in mind—a thought best caught in the Westminster Catechism: "Man's chief aim is to glorify God and to enjoy him forever."

The currency at stake here is, who is the initiator in life—God or man? Many modern Christians have adapted the popular motivational speakers' views of the human person: We dream and then do *whatever* we want to. And we expect God to bless it, to make it great.

The human agenda is caught in an old song, "The Impossible Dream." The lyrics speak of daring to dream impossible dreams, beating all foes, overcoming undearable sorrow, and running smack into the face of whatever life throws at us—no matter how hopeless. It's a "who-cares-how-far, just-follow-the-star" philosophy. Why? Because we humans can. We're just that good.

We are big on the biblical text "I can do all things" (Phil. 4:13 KJV). But the Bible warns about this. We are told not to run impulsively with our own plans, because our life is "a mist that appears for a little while and then vanishes" (James 4:14). We are here for too short a time to cultivate enough wisdom to make life decisions on our own. "Instead," the text goes, "you ought to say, 'If it is the Lord's will, we will live and do this or that'" (v. 15). That means that you and I can play a significant role, but we don't get to write our own play. We are in God's story; He should initiate or at least carry the right of veto on life's plans.

Many church people carry their own agendas and cultivate self-actualizing dreams, believing that if they just add a dab of faith to their dreaming, they may receive from God the extra "luck" they need to get the fame, power, and wealth that they want. It is true that the Scriptures teach, "Everything is possible for him who believes" (Mark 9:23). But if we are not careful, the whole thing ends up being just a stone's throw from God's being reduced to our *Servant.* Our own desires quickly become the center of the universe. This is great brand of American Christianity, but it isn't the biblical kind.

3. *He will complete what He started in us.* The apostle Paul wrote, "There has never been the slightest doubt in my mind that the God who started this great work in you would keep at it and bring it to a flourishing finish on the very day Christ Jesus appears" (Phil. 1:6 MSG). You gotta love this. God promises to keep chasing us and working in us even after we start our journey of faith.

This is great news, because the thing we tend to do best is botch things. God forgives us; we fall again. God gives us courage; we get discouraged. God gives us a dream; we make it a self-actualizing quest filled more with us than God. God gives us gifts; we go prodigal with them and use them for our own advantage. Let's face it; if we were God, we would kill us.

The wonderful news is that God knows us completely and still loves us. J. I. Packer writes, "There is tremendous relief in knowing that his love to me is utterly realistic, based at every point on prior knowledge of the worst about me, so that no discovery now can disillusion him about me, in the way I am so often disillusioned about myself."[1]

God bases His decision to pursue us and work in us on His unconditional love. Unconditional love loves *without* conditions—it isn't based on the actions of the one being loved. This God-kind of love simply sets value and preciousness on us. It isn't an earned thing; it just *is*. We are loved because *we are*. We belong because *we are*. When this truth becomes real to you, there is no more fear of abandonment. In fact, this "perfect love drives out fear" (1 John 4:18).

Virginia Lively tells of a vision she once had of Jesus Christ that gives us a snapshot of this kind of love. She writes, "[The] thing that struck me was his utter lack of condemnation. I realized at once that he knew me down to my very marrow. He knew all the stupid, cruel, silly things I had ever done. But I also realized that none of these things—nothing I could ever do—would alter the absolute caring, the unconditional love that I saw in his eyes. I could not grasp it! It was too immense a fact. I felt that if I gazed at him for a thousand years, I still could not realize the enormity of that love."[2]

I have no idea why, but God loves us. He believes in us. He trusts us. He pursues us. When we see that, really *remember* that, we can't help but love Him. "We love [Him] because he first loved us" (1 John 4:19).

WHO WE ARE

It is important to remember who we are apart from Jesus Christ—*losers*. But it is more important to remember who we are because of our *connection* to Jesus Christ—"more than conquerors!" (Rom. 8:37). God did a miracle inside us when we opened our hearts and started on the journey of faith. The Bible says our very nature, our essence, changed. "Therefore, if anyone is in Christ, he is a new creation; the old has gone, the new has come!" (2 Cor. 5:17). That means there is a part of our beings that has been transformed—made new.

Concerning this: God said, "I will give you a new heart and put a new spirit in you; I will remove from you your heart of stone and give you a heart of flesh" (Eze. 36:26–27). This miracle has happened inside us. *That* was the difference we felt when we asked Jesus to become part of our lives. God took out the *old* us and put in a *new* us. We are different people than we used to be. We are new creations!

This miracle is so deep that sometimes it may not dramatically touch your emotions. Don't be concerned about that. Many don't *feel* much different after coming to Christ, but they eventually realize that they have new longings and priorities. The greatness of this miracle is *not* determined by how much *feeling* you have. You may not *feel* anything spectacular or out of the ordinary, but you will notice a difference in your life. For instance, before coming to Christ you may have felt a *little guilty* about saying or doing bad things. Now you are going to discover a much stronger reaction in your heart. You will find yourself being very sensitive to the wrong that you do—you will hate it. The reason is, you have a new nature now. The old part of you that was devoted to sin has been replaced. It is as though you have been born all over again.

And that is exactly what happened as you came to Jesus and entered the kingdom, or *influence*, of God. Jesus said, "I tell you the truth, no one can see the kingdom of God unless he is born again" (John 3:3).

Now you won't feel comfortable getting angry with people or talking ugly about them. You won't feel good about destroying your body with drugs or alcohol. You won't let yourself follow the passions and lusts that you knew before coming to Christ. Sex with someone to whom you are not married will stop. This won't happen because you decided to become a goody-goody, but because God's nature of purity has been deposited into your new, recreated "heart." This does not mean you will never slip back into the old ways to which you were accustomed. It means that when you do, you will not feel comfortable with it—you will long to make things right again. Before coming to Christ, it was never such a big deal to sin— your reasoning went something like, *After all, I am only human.*

That reasoning won't work anymore, because you are no longer just human—now you are a child of God. You are different, and you know it. Because of His presence in your life, you will sense His displeasure whenever you fall back into sin, and you will want to distance yourself from the sin instead of from Him. If you do find yourself slipping back into old sin patterns, just call upon Jesus again.

Jesus promised to help us when we are tempted to return to wrong patterns of living. When He physically left this planet, He did not intend to leave us struggling on our own. He said, "I will not leave you as orphans; I will come to you" (John 14:18). If you get tricked and find yourself back in sin, run to Jesus. He will cleanse you again and again when you fail. Scripture says, "If we confess our sins, he is faithful and just and will forgive us our sins and purify us from all unrighteousness" (1 John 1:9). Jesus is faithful to forgive us, no matter *how often* we fail Him through sin.

Knowing this will keep your faith strong through failure while you are still learning how to live in a new way. It takes time to learn how to break off Satan's influence in your life, so don't get discouraged. You don't have to be perfect. God just wants you to grow.

Because of this *born-again* experience, on some metaphysical level, what is true of Christ is now true of us. The Bible claims we are "united with Christ" (Phil. 2:1) and we share His image (1 John 4:17). He is now part of our identity. But what does that *really* mean?

It means in some mystical way that we are literally tucked into Christ and all that He is. The Bible repeatedly says we are "in Christ" (2 Cor. 5:17) or "in him" (Eph. 1:4). As a result of being connected with Jesus Christ, there is something deep inside us that is able to resist sin (Rom. 6:14); that longs to love God and people (Rom. 5:5); that is kind, forgiving, patient, good, faithful, gentle, and self-controlled (Gal. 5:22); and that is full of righteousness, holiness, and wisdom (1 Cor. 1:30). Actually, anything you can say about Jesus, you can say about us, *because* Jesus has chosen to live *inside* of us! (Rev. 3:20). Paul said the amazing "mystery" about Christianity is "Christ in you" (Col. 1:27).

But when we look *away* from Jesus and *toward* self, all we find is the remains of the Fall—that which the Bible calls the *old self*. Paul wrote, "With regard to your former way of life . . . *put off your old self* . . . and . . . *put on the new self*, created to be like God in true righteousness and holiness" (Eph. 4:22, 24, emphasis added). When we look away from the *old self* and unto Jesus Christ, we discover our new identities, our *new selves*. That is why the Scripture commands us to "fix our eyes on Jesus" (Heb. 12:2).

The whole concept of Christian living is that we don't act to *become*; we *are*—therefore, we *act*. We are able to act, not because we are good, but because *He* who is good, lives in and through us. He is our new identity! As long as our eyes are on Him and off of ourselves, we can experience a level of life and holiness that is impossible otherwise.

How much of His life we enjoy, how much of His power and position we experience is not dependent on *how* we look by our performance, but on *where* we look. Our new identity is not based upon what we accomplish *for* Christ but on what God accomplished *in* Christ *for us*. When we turn away from and reject *self* and turn to Jesus, we begin an eye-opening discovery of a new identity in Him. This self-abnegation is vital to experiencing new life in Christ.

Now we don't answer the "Who am I?" question the same way we used to. We no longer have to create ourselves through "positive thinking." We no longer have to *become* somebody by gaining power, influence, fame, or fortune. The old way of living is gone.

The list below (which is far from exhaustive) presents in first-person who we really are now that we are *in Christ*. These are the lofty traits we were *born* with when we were *born again*. We cannot earn them any more than a baby can earn legs, eyes, ears, or a brain—that stuff comes in the package of being born human. Similarly, these exalted traits belong to anyone who is "born of God" (John 1:13).

OUR DNA IN CHRIST

I am a new creation, created in Christ Jesus, with "new" things from God on the inside of me. (2 Cor. 5:17–18)

I have "died" to the influence of the first Adam (Col. 3:3) and am now "alive in Christ." (Rom. 6:11)

I am righteous and holy. (Rom. 5:17; Eph. 4:24)

Sin no longer has power over me. (Rom. 6:1–6)

I have the honor of being seated with Christ in heavenly realms. (Eph. 2:6)

I have the full righteousness, holiness, and wisdom of Jesus Christ. (1 Cor. 1:30)

I have the mind of Christ. (1 Cor. 2:16)

I am forever free from condemnation. (Rom. 8:1)

God is now my Father, and I am His child. (1 John 3:1)

God is *for* me, and no one can successfully stand against me. (Rom. 8:31)

He has chosen and adopted me, and I am blameless in His eyes. (Eph. 1:4–5)

With Jesus, I am more than a conqueror. (Rom. 8:37)

I can do all things through Christ who strengthens me. (Phil. 4:13)

God will turn things around in my life to work for my good. (Rom. 8:28)

I have become a temple of God. (1 Cor. 6:19)

Christ actually dwells in me. (Col. 1:27)

I am the salt of the earth. (Matt. 5:13)

I am the light of the world. (Matt. 5:14)

As He is, so am I in this world. (1 John 4:17)

I am a friend of God. (John 15:15)

I am a member of Christ's body. (1 Cor. 12:27; Eph. 5:30)

I am a saint. (Eph. 1:1, 18; Phil. 1:1)

I am a citizen of heaven. (Phil. 3:20)

I am a child of light and not of darkness. (1 Thess. 5:5)

I am a partaker of Christ; I share His life and heavenly calling. (Heb. 3:1, 14)

I am a member of a chosen race, a royal priesthood, a holy nation, a people for God's own possession. (1 Peter 2:9)

I have been bought with a price; I am not my own; I belong to God. (1 Cor. 6:19–20)

I have been established, anointed, and sealed by God in Christ. (2 Cor. 1:21–22)

I have been given the Holy Spirit as a pledge guaranteeing my inheritance to come. (Eph. 1:13–14)

I have been blessed with every spiritual blessing. (Eph. 1:3)

I was predestined—determined by God—to be adopted as God's child. (Eph. 1:5)

I have direct access to God through the Spirit. (Eph. 2:18)

I have been redeemed and forgiven of all my sins. The debt against me has been canceled. (Col. 1:14)

I am firmly rooted in Christ and am now being built up in Him. (Col. 2:7)

I have been rescued from the dominion of Satan and transferred to the kingdom of Christ. (Col. 1:13)

I have been made complete in Christ. (Col. 2:10)

I am His workmanship and am now able to do good works. (Eph. 2:10)

I have been given everything I need to live a godly life. (2 Peter 1:3)

I have been given a spirit of power, love, and self-discipline. (2 Tim. 1:7)

I have been given God's exceedingly great and precious promises, by which I am a partaker of God's divine nature. (2 Peter 1:4)

This is our new identity! These are the cold, hard facts of our new life in Christ. We did not earn any of this—that is why it is called grace. These are the things *God has accomplished in Christ.* As long as our eyes are on Him and off of ourselves, we can enjoy and identify with all that is in Jesus.

MIRRORS DON'T LIE

Though I don't anymore, I wore a mustache for several years. Throughout the day I would pull on it with my fingers and probe it with my tongue. I liked my "stache"—but Gail never did. She said it "poked" her when I kissed her. My mother hated it too. She said it made me look like a "bandito." I finally broke down and shaved.

When I did, I couldn't believe how funny my upper lip looked when I first peered into the mirror. For some time, when I'd look in the mirror, expecting to see myself one way, there was this *new guy* looking back. But since mirrors don't lie, I had to accept the new me. After a period of time (*mirror* time), I got used to my new ID. I eventually quit trying to play with my absent mustache and even became familiar with the face I saw.

The same is certainly true for our new identity in Jesus! Most of us have never thought of ourselves in any way other than from our own historical contexts. We see ourselves based upon our upbringing, our experiences, our personal strengths and weaknesses. When we begin looking into the "mirror" of God's Word (James 1:23), we don't recognize the *new guy* looking back at us as *being* us! But mirrors don't lie; you really are new in Christ (2 Cor. 5:17)!

TRUE CORRECTION

The real test of whether you are viewing yourself accurately is by how you view correction.

When Michelangelo was queried about how he carved the life-size image of King David, from one large stone, he replied, "I just cut away everything that didn't look like David." Something in that story captures the essence of correction. When we correct someone, we are not correcting that person's actions to *make* him or her into a "David"; we are cutting away everything that is *anti*-David—we are trying to uncover the *David* that is *already there*.

Did you ever notice how the European royals act? Their stately walk, the way they hold their heads, their manners? Where did they learn to act that way? Certainly they didn't emerge from the womb with that level of finesse and etiquette. No, they were trained. But *how* were they trained? When they acted unbecomingly, did a nanny or their parents scream at them, "You'll never be royalty if you don't stop acting that way!"

I strongly doubt it.

I bet you would have heard something more like, "Young man, you are a prince. One day you will be king. Princes and kings do not act the way you are acting. You must act in concert with your station. You are who you are. You cannot change that. *Act* like who you are!"

Correction that honors one's personhood while challenging her to rise to a higher place demonstrates an accurate understanding of a Christian's station. When Paul addressed the saints in Corinth who were falling in and out of serious sin, he didn't berate them or threaten them with "If you want to be Christians, you better stop doing all that bad stuff!" No. He said to them, "Do you not know" that "you are not your own" and that "you were bought at a price?" (1 Cor. 6:19–20).

He was challenging them to remember *who they were* so they could then begin to act in concert with who they were. Christianity isn't about *becoming* by doing good; it's about *being* who you have become in Christ. We don't need to attack people when we correct them; we need to urge them to be what God intended and then do what we can to "chisel" away what doesn't look like who God says they are. This helps us focus on attacking the problems people have, not the people who have them.

When I was about eight years old, I was playing in a Little League softball game. I was terrible. I was up to bat and swung just in time for my fingers to get slammed by the ball. I choked back my tears and set up for the next pitch. I swung again and got hit in the exact same place on my hand. I started to cry openly, which was extremely embarrassing in front of my friends. I remember running off the field in absolute humiliation. My mom met me in the parking lot, grabbed my face, looked directly into my eyes, and said, "Don't you worry one bit about not doing well at baseball. You're a Gungor."

At the moment, I didn't know what she meant by that, but there was something in her voice that communicated to me that I was bigger than failure. Her confidence in me despite my open failure felt like a healing ooze flowing into me to let me know I was OK, no matter what. She made me believe I mattered, not because of what I had done, but because of who I *was*. By the time I grew up enough to know that being a Gungor meant *absolutely nothing at all,* the healing salve had already permeated my soul—I had a healthy self-image and a strong sense of destiny that made me smile at the future. What a gift! (Thanks, Mom.)

Remembering to remember *who God is* and *who we are* is hard work. Our minds naturally default to other things. But remembering is a huge part of faith. If we don't remember, we *drift* into spiritual amnesia.

19

the charley horse:
when "get to" becomes "got to"

I love innocence. It's both dangerous and wonderful. Innocence is purity without corruption. It's jammed with trust and curiosity, without ever considering the possible positive or negative outcomes of an action. A toddler running out into the street, chasing a butterfly, is an example of innocence at work. That's why innocence is only safe in the company of wisdom. But there is a raw, wonderful quality about being *willing* to wander out into the street without fear or agenda— just because of innocent curiosity, or because of a complete trust that *another* is responsible to watch our backs.

In general, I think we need more curiosity and trust, and less being cool and being know-it-alls. As believers, we should stay innocent and trusting and curious about God and life. Innocence loves to learn—*needs* to learn. We must never stop being learners. Jesus told us not to call anyone "teacher" because we "have one Teacher, the Christ" (Matt. 23:10). I think He was saying that humans need to be forever humble, open, and learning. We need to ask more questions and listen more often. The Bible itself says we should be "quick to listen" and "slow to speak" (James 1:19).

INNOCENCE FOSTERS FRUITFULNESS

There is an amazing Old Testament story about some guys and some sticks. The sticks were called *staffs*, and they were pretty handy in that agrarian culture. People used them to walk over rugged terrain, to poke and manage their livestock, and to beat back wolves—both the animal and human kind.

God was looking for a tribe within the twelve tribes of Israel to administrate the duties of temple worship. So He told Moses to gather the "staffs" of the leaders from each of these tribes and to carve their names on their sticks. Moses was to lay the staffs before God overnight. God told Moses He would show which tribe was chosen through a supernatural sign—the dead stick of the chosen tribe would grow leaves and foliage overnight.

The next morning, Moses "saw that Aaron's staff, which represented the house of Levi, had not only sprouted but had budded, blossomed and produced almonds" (Num. 17:8).

How cool is that?

Imagine being one of those tribal leaders. They had to be wondering what was going to happen—curiosity was piqued. But they just obeyed, which is what trust looks like. The only one in control here was God. No one was manipulating or maneuvering results. They just watched wide-eyed to see what God would do. This is innocence. And the result was miraculous: God moved. Something changed. What was dead began to produce.

I would rather *produce* than be dead. I like the idea of supernatural growth being a part of my life and faith. I'm suggesting that innocence is necessary for that. I think God wants us to lay our daily lives—the stuff we do and things we use (our *staffs*)—in reckless abandon before Him, and then stand back, brimming with curiosity and trust—*innocence*. Just chase the butterfly.

God doesn't want us to try to manipulate and control outcomes.

We bring to *Him* our dead human activity; *He* causes it to bud and sprout with spiritual life. We trust Him; the fruit of God comes; we produce spiritual almonds that can feed the world. Good times.

I can think of dozens of stories in my own life and in the lives of those with whom I have shared life where we walked into the prayer place, laid our "staff" before God, and just hung there . . . maybe for weeks. But eventually, something started to bud and sprout, and fruit came.

I remember when I traveled with a group known as the Jesus People back in the early 1970s. One night we all began singing together spontaneously, without instruments. Some sang in English; others sang in their prayer language (*glossolalia*). It was an amazing spiritual experience—a new kind of worship encounter. No one planned it. Our curiosity and love for God caused us to stumble into it. It was supernatural.

If you go back to the origins of any significant ministry or mission's effort, you will find someone innocently calling out to God. Then somewhere along the way he or she stumbles upon an idea that sort of *blossoms* from within. Almond production. This is the way of God. It brings excitement and hope—it's the thing we call *vision*. When it comes, there is a supernatural energy that helps us face what looks like insurmountable odds. We press through with the joy that we *get to* do something with God. This is innocence. It's easy to breathe when things are innocent, and life is fun.

I stumbled into pastoral care this way. I didn't want to be a preacher. I hated the idea of taking up offerings (still do). But as I came to God in church, in prayer, and in worship—without agenda, in innocence—I began to feel a stirring. Then the thought, *I want you to preach*, bloomed in me.

I really didn't know what to do with it, but as I continued to keep my life before God, fruit began to come. Without my orchestrating or manipulating anything, people started to listen to me.

Wherever I went, I would start talking and people would tune in. They would tell me they wanted to hear more. I was passing out *spiritual almonds.*

I began teaching publicly because I didn't have time to follow up on all the personal conversations I was having. The "public thing" was done to simplify ministry, not to market it. There was no care for money or ministry size or popularity—I just wanted to help people—innocently. But innocence is hard to maintain.

WHEN "GET TO" BECOMES "GOT TO"

The truth is, we often become victims of what innocence brings us. We start chasing the butterfly, but we get run over. After a few nights of open worship with the Jesus People, we quickly moved from the notion that we *"get to"* worship this way, to we *"got to"* worship this way (*got tos* are bad things). Instead of running at God and not caring about outcomes—stumbling into open worship or not—we felt we had to recapture what we had experienced; we began to force the issue. Our "get to" became a "got to." *Got tos* are like knots in the human soul—a kind of spiritual *charley horse.*

In my own pastoral ministry the "got tos" found footing. I started out great. I was loving God, loving God-thoughts, loving God's people, and having fun. Our meetings were growing in size, and people were excited about what God was doing. But then, as with everywhere else in life, the season of growth was followed by a season of winter; things slowed down.

Instead of ignoring what was going on and continuing to foster my unabashed, innocent pursuit of God, I started to think, *Why aren't things growing as well? What am I doing wrong? I've got to get this right. I've* got to *do something to keep the momentum."* The more "got tos" that flooded my thinking, the more my spiritual muscles cramped up in typical charley-horse fashion. My butterfly turned to goo on somebody's windshield, as I lay crippled in pain on the pavement.

So much of what we call ministry and Christian living seems to be more "got to" than "get to." We start out full of curiosity and trust, but somewhere along the way, things go south. When I survey most of the followers of Jesus I know (even leaders), they seem less like innocent kids having a blast on a playground or in a pool on a hot summer afternoon, and more like zombies from *Night of the Living Dead*; they are moving, but it ain't pretty. Where is the abundant life Jesus talked about (John 10:10 KJV)?

When we lose innocence, we lose life, and we become victims of our past experiences—experiences that were first born out of joyful innocence.

FAKE ALMONDS

Victims always make adjustments. When we become victims of something we innocently stumbled into, we start to fake it. Imagine being Aaron, with the harvest of ripe almonds from his staff. Those almonds appeared *only* after there was sufficient "laying before God" time. But what did Aaron do when he ran out of them? Presumably, he would have taken his staff back to the presence of God and kept it there until more reappeared.

But if we abandon our "laying before God" time, and only spend our time developing a marketing plan for our almonds—developing the packaging, creating the artwork, and forming the ad campaign— we will stop producing real almonds. And if the demand for the almonds of ministry remains high (especially if people ran into real ones from us before), we will believe we've *got to* produce almonds that we no longer have. Hence, we start producing fake ones.

Fake joy. Fake praise and worship. Fake ministry. Fake smiles. Fake love. Fake brokenness. Fake expressions. Fake concern. Fake holiness. Fake *life*.

When I was about four, I remember going over to a lady's house with my mom. There was a bowl of delicious grapes on the table in front of me, calling for me to eat them, but I was too shy to ask if I could have one. My opportunity came when the two women went into another room: I seized one. I popped it in my mouth and began to masticate. *Errugh-uh, errugh-uh, errugh-uh,* was the sound that ensued.

Something was wrong. This was 1959, and these grapes were *rubber*. I had never seen rubber grapes before. They totally faked me out.

I think lots of people in Christian life and ministry are putting out rubber grapes. They used to have real ones; but no longer. The fakes look good—perfect really, but they go *"errugh-uh"* when you try to chew on what they offer, and they have zero nutritional value. Even good fakes are still fake.

Sadly, I have given way to being fake as a pastor.

I remember walking out of my office and running into Pete in the hall. He was a young, energetic guy who was just discovering the joys of prayer and was dreaming about making a commitment to ministry. He pulled me aside and said, "Pastor, I just had the coolest thing happen in prayer . . . "

Instead of sharing his excitement, I felt myself get upset. I don't know if I was jealous of him or what. But I definitely felt *less*. For weeks I had been working on church-building and staff issues and had felt my soul getting pale, see-throughish, really. I needed a God-break. I should have said to Pete, "That's great! Would you mind praying for me right now? I have been so busy and haven't had any great God-time. I feel like I have been eating 'carnal corn' and I need some of what's on you to get on me."

But that would have meant admitting I wasn't where I should be. And I was the leader. I felt I needed to keep up my image. So instead of confessing any weakness or neediness, I snapped off a couple of

Bible verses about prayer and told him of an experience or two I had had in the past, which made his experience seem just a little *less* dramatic. I one-upped him pretty good—but got all knotted up inside— I got a huge internal charley horse. Fake always does that.

I think we need to stop the madness and get real. We need to be honest when we're spiritually pale and say, "I think I'm backslid. I think I need more God time." We need to wear signs around our necks that say, No Almonds Today, unless there *really are*.

If we are going to reach a Christless world, we need to come up with the real deal. No one is expecting you to be fruitful 365 days a year—nothing in nature does that. Even God "sabbathed"—no fruit that day. Most are delighted when we are vulnerable about what's going on in our souls.

Sadly, some will try to use your honesty against you. There are those who feel they need to gain approval and applause from others by living life *big*—bigger than it really is. Like the Wizard in *Wizard of Oz*, they hide behind a curtain and pull levers that make themselves appear larger-than-life on a big screen. They would rather promote the illusion of being powerful and in control than admit that they lack almonds. Until the truth is revealed, until someone pulls away the curtain, they pretend to be bigger than they are. (Where is Toto when you need him?)

But fighting for innocence is still worth it. And innocence is what keeps us childlike in our faith (Jesus said in Matthew 18:3 that the kingdom was totally built for kids).

And it makes God smile.

THE CURE

Coming in real contact with the Almighty is a thing of tension. You can't help but tap into the idea that more is possible. You catch glimpses of possibilities that are so much bigger than you that it's easy to get lost in the thinking of them. If you are not careful, you will stop thinking *I get to do this* and become a victim of doing it.

Whether you are trying to be a good mom or dad or friend or missionary, you stand to burn out from doing too much of a good thing. There is a thin red line between doing what you do innocently and with joy and being overwhelmed with what should be done, which quickly leads to an internal knotting of your limited human soul.

I have a friend who just wanted to do something for God that was practical and helpful to people. He stumbled into the God-idea of helping hurting single moms by fixing up their apartments and homes. He rallied young folks to participate and businesses to give him huge discounts for supplies and furniture. Cool deal. And they went hog wild. They were having a blast.

But recently I heard the tone of his voice change. The "get to" help has become "got to" help, and now he is more aware of how much *more* needs to be done. It is more than he and his group are able to do. He has even taken on the task of trying to get others to own the idea as well. Great thoughts. But if he is not careful, he will become a victim of what began as an innocent ministry to help people. It will become a burden much bigger than he can bear.

That's the way this God stuff works. We tap into the Being of God. He is unlimited and all powerful. If we are not careful, we will think that, because of our association with Him, we are too.

Thankfully, there are ways to make sure ministry and Christian living stay in the "get to" versus "got to" zone—ways to stay full of curiosity and trust, while loving and enjoying what you are doing. But you must ask yourself the right questions to discover the right answers. Let me give you four.

1. *Am I willing to allow another person to do what I think I must do?* If you say no, that is an indicator that your identity is too wrapped

up in what you are doing and that you trust yourself more than God. When I examine what I feel called to do and I ask myself this question, I run into a litany of mixed feelings inside. Some of these are attached to the idea that I'm the *only one* who can do what God is asking of me, which makes me feel unique and special. But if that ideology goes unchecked, I am only doing it because I want to *matter*. Then I become a victim of my longing to matter, not an innocent servant who only wants to see God glorified. If I only want God to be glorified, I won't care who does it.

But sometimes I don't want anyone else to do it because it's *mine*—I own it. I run at my calling because I don't want anyone else to. I become a slave to my perceived duty because of the inner dragons of envy and jealousy. No hint of innocence here.

Unless we can agree to letting someone else do the dream we feel we have from God, we are not spiritually fit to do it—we are not innocent enough to do it in a way that honors God.

2. *Am I willing to do what I am doing, even if no one else knows I am doing it?* If you cannot answer yes to this (and God will test you on these points), you are plagued with an improper, self-promoting agenda that precludes innocence.
3. *Am I willing to have others copy me and not give me any credit?* That is a horrifying thought to the noninnocent.
4. *Am I willing to let God use me for a season, and then be OK with Him later putting my work into the hands of another?*

John the Baptist experienced this. He was the one who announced the coming of Messiah, Jesus. Jesus was John's cousin, and He came on the scene when John was in the heyday of his ministry. People were coming to John by the thousands. But after John said, "Behold the Lamb of God!" (John 1:36 KJV) and baptized Jesus, people stopped following John and started following Jesus.

John's disciples came and told him that all the people were now going to Jesus' meetings. The facts were: the crowds were down, offerings were down, and John had become the "five-minutes-ago" man.

John's response was telling. He said, "A man can receive only what is given him from heaven" (John 3:27). Then he said, "He must become greater; I must become less" (v. 30).

Years ago, when I first began pastoring, a lady who was an amazing orator spoke in our church. Everyone loved her. In fact, I felt completely threatened by how much our church members loved her. In a kind of internal huff, I decided I wasn't going to have any special speakers in for a while. I spiritualized the decision, but it was really just raw fear and insecurity.

A short time later, I ran into this story about John and Jesus. I felt the Holy Spirit nudging me to rethink how I was to be involved with the lives of others. I seemed to hear, *Ed, you have what you have because God has given it to you. No one can take the influence God has given you.* I had to repent of the fear that someone was going to steal people from me. I instantly knew I needed to be open to God's using others in our midst—visitors or members—without being threatened. We immediately began to build a culture of "come here and shine," instead of "stand back so Pastor Ed can shine."

That same day I also heard the Holy Spirit say, *You only want to trust God to cause you to become greater. But it takes more faith to become less in others' lives after you have influenced them than it does to influence them to begin with.*

It was true. I only prayed for more influence. But the Spirit's voice helped me understand that sometimes God gives us influence in the lives of others, and then He takes it away. He was urging me not to be afraid of that, but to trust God through it. It's obviously much harder to shrink than to grow—our culture doesn't define success by how much less you are this year.

But alternating seasons of growing influence and loss of influence are present in everything from friendships to raising kids—there are seasons when we greatly influence others and seasons when that influence wanes.

LET'S REVIEW

Now, let's ask ourselves these questions one more time:

1. *Am I willing to allow another person to do what I think I must do?*
2. *Am I willing to do what I am doing, even if no one else knows I am doing it?*
3. *Am I willing to have others copy me and not give me any credit?*
4. *Am I willing to let God use me for a season, and then be OK with Him later putting my work into the hands of another?*

Only by embracing innocence can we keep saying yes—and avoid charley-horsing our souls.

20

color blindness:
only dreams come in black and white

It is said that people dream in black and white. But the real world is in living color. Remember the movie *Pleasantville?* In the universe of Pleasantville (filmed in black and white instead of color), life was . . . pleasant. Nothing akin to the horrors of war, famine, or AIDS existed there. The bathrooms didn't even have toilets—that would have been impolite. The high-school basketball team never missed a shot, firemen only rescued cats stuck in trees (there were no house fires), families were perfect, and teen sweethearts never went past "first base." Everything, absolutely everything, was perfect in that idyllic little town.

In Pleasantville everything was simple and clear. Black-and-white ruled. But as the citizens of Pleasantville began to explore the joys and choices of life, things started turning from black-and-white to color—first a flower, then the surroundings, then people. But with the appearance of color came the dark side of human nature. That's the danger with color—it comes with the potential of good *and* evil. In response, some in Pleasantville were willing to do *whatever* to maintain the status quo, to maintain their simple black-and-white world. Their fear and paranoia led to intolerance, hate crimes, and violence against anything *colored*.

175

THE COMPLEXITY OF COLOR

Color is more complex than black and white, which is probably why we like to talk about life as though it were black-and-white simple. For instance, role-playing is pretty black-and-white, certainly less complex than intimacy. Intimacy is about *knowing* and *being known*. Role-playing has nothing to do with the complexity of understanding one another; it's about doing one's job. Many husbands and wives don't really know or understand each other. He is the husband; she is the wife. Many children and parents don't know each other either. Kids act out their role as kids; and parents act out their role as parents. The truth is, knowing and understanding one another is much harder than playing a role. Role-playing is black-and-white simple.

Lots of folks try to make faith a black-and-white issue, but it's not. It is filled with complexity. I believe in God most of the time. Sometimes I am red-hot in love with Him. Other times I resemble the heat of a skillet that was *recently* red-hot—there is a rumor of warmth. And at still other times, I get scared that I might not believe in God at all—I'm just going through some religious motions. Yet something in me keeps pulling me toward belief, and I realize I really *do* believe in God. Messy stuff. I guess faith comes in color.

When it comes to discovering truth, most parents and spiritual leaders prefer black and white and resist complexity. Complexity is too colorful. We prefer doling out black-and-white conclusions. Telling people *what* seems so much simpler than telling them *why*. And safer too. Thinking, cognizing, conceptualizing, perceiving, understanding, comprehending, and cogitating—all are words for actions that are much more complex than simply commanding and directing. Commanding our kids to act in a certain way is so clean, so black-and-white simple. Helping them internalize the *why* behind an action (at an appropriate age) and letting them participate in a discussion on conclusions is both cumbersome and potentially dangerous—they may conclude something different than we parents and leaders do. *God forbid.*

TO DANCE OR NOT TO DANCE

Jeff was a teenager when he talked with me about his dancing problem back in the late 1970s. He was a new Christian and came to me wide-eyed because he had just heard that dancing was a sin. He loved dancing (discotheques were extremely popular back then).

He asked me straight up, "Is it a sin to dance?"

I was a member of a church that had labeled dancing a "worldly" activity and forbade it completely (the prohibition was in small print on our membership cards). So when Jeff asked, I found myself beginning to say, "Of course." But just as I started to speak, I felt something in my heart checking the pat answer I had always given. I paused for a split second; abandoned my oversimplified, rigid position; and took what I understood to be God's position, though it was messier and less direct than I preferred. I said, "The Bible really doesn't say, 'Don't dance,' but it does teach us not to call attention to ourselves in inappropriate ways. We are not supposed to try to be Mr. Cool or to act in seductive ways. Sometimes dancing is all about those things, and that's why some would say it is a sin.

"So, let me ask you," I continued, "are you planning on going dancing again soon?"

"Yes, this Thursday night," he replied.

"Well," I suggested, "when you go out on the dance floor, watch what's going on in your heart. If you can go out and have fun and not be lewd or Mr. Cool, and if you can worship God while you're out there—go for it, man. If not, quit dancing."

I'd be lying to you if I told you I didn't get nervous. I did. Abandoning my black-and-white deductions and opening the door for Jeff to process truth felt so unsafe. Had I opened Pandora's box? I had to trust Jeff and the Holy Spirit—who I *hoped* was the one who told me to answer Jeff's question in this way.

I saw him about a week later, and his first words were, "I can't go dancing anymore."

"Why not?" I asked, relieved that I hadn't made him more "worldly."

"I just felt dirty," he said. "I found myself trying to impress and hit on girls. It wasn't good."

The Jeff event showed me that we can dare to give truth to people in the same way God gives it to us—messy and not so full of absolutes. Though the truth remains the same for all of us, God trusts us to wrestle with it till it makes sense *for us*. Perhaps that is why Paul penned, "One man considers one day more sacred than another; another man considers every day alike. Each one should be fully convinced in his own mind" (Rom. 14:5). How cool is that? God believes in us and in His ability to interact with us. He allows the higgledy-piggledy of our humanness into the mix of sorting things through and applying them in a way that builds and strengthens us. Some of us will come to different conclusions, but that is OK. Perhaps life is to be experienced in living color.

But living in color means we must allow room for differences. That means that sometimes it may be OK for Christians to dance.

When Gail and I began pastoring in central Wisconsin, a couple in the church asked me to perform their wedding ceremony. It was our first *big* wedding in that rural culture.

All went well until we got to the reception. Everyone started dancing—many of them our parishioners. Gail and I looked at each other, trying to decide whether we should stay or bolt in order to make a statement discouraging this "worldly" behavior.

Up to that point we were opposed to dancing. But now something was different. The best we could tell, these dancing folks weren't being lewd or weird—they were just having fun. We watched for a while, and when we decided this was no cover-up for evil, I grabbed Gail, and we went out on that forbidden floor. We had a total blast.

We still dance.

Dangerous. That's all you can say about steering away from black-and-white. Don't misunderstand me. There are plenty of absolutes given in Scripture: the Ten Commandments, for example. But there are many areas where God just gives us parameters, not absolutes, and He affords us the space to work within those parameters. He doesn't always give us a loaf of bread. Often He gives us the raw ingredients (flour, yeast, salt, oil, etc.), and we can make either bread or pizza crust, leavened or unleavened. As long as we do not add some harmful ingredient (like a sinful motive), we can enjoy choice and still live within the parameters of holy living.

GOD TRUSTS US

I think God trusts us more than we realize. When Jesus prayed to the Father just before His Passion, it is amazing that He didn't beg God for more time. The crowds that had followed Him scattered, the Twelve were about to abandon Him after His arrest (and He knew it), and there was no strategic plan for forming and growing the Church. Still, Jesus simply prayed, "I have brought you glory on earth by completing the work you gave me to do" (John 17:4). What was He thinking?

Jesus had told His disciples He was going to die. And they got depressed. Who was going to lead them? Who would tell them what to do? Jesus replied, "I tell you the truth: It is for your good that I am going away" (John 16:7). Why? Because He said that the Holy Spirit would come, and "when he, the Spirit of truth, comes, he will guide you into all truth" (John 16:13). Jesus wasn't panicking, because He knew these guys would get connected with the Holy Spirit. I think Jesus was OK with the messiness of incarnation—the God-and-human mix. He knew the Holy Spirit would "guide" them and fill their lives with truth.

> John takes the same position. He writes to believers, "But you have received the Holy Spirit, and he lives within you, so you don't need anyone to teach you what is true. For the Spirit teaches you all things, and what he teaches is true" (1 John 2:27 NLT).

Whoa. *We don't need anyone to teach us?* Before you fall off your chair, let me assure you that He is *not* saying we shouldn't teach the Bible or tell people the truth. He is saying we must respect people's ability to think and the Holy Spirit's role in weaving truth into the human soul. But that requires trusting God in people. The problem with that is, not everyone consistently submits to God's working in his or her life, and that means there will be error.

Did you ever notice how much time the New Testament writers spent on correcting erroneous thinking and sinful actions? If the writers had just listed a boatload of dos and don'ts, it would have eliminated much of that. But it would have also eliminated freedom.

Freedom is a funny thing. The power to be free is also the power to be wrong. Some have wondered why God gave Adam and Eve the power to sin. The best answer I've heard is that the power to choose right is the same power to choose evil. It is the power of *choice*, period. Sometimes I think that, in our quest to eliminate evil, we inadvertently eliminate the power to choose at all.

Paul declares, "It is for freedom that Christ has set us free" (Gal. 5:1). But then he warns, "But do not use your freedom to indulge the sinful nature" (v. 13). If we decide to honor people's right to think and to choose, we need to be OK with challenging them when they use their freedom as a cover-up for sinful agendas. This is untidy stuff. You can feel the tension as Paul tries to encourage responsible living without robbing Christian freedom: "'Everything is permissible'—

but not everything is beneficial. 'Everything is permissible'—but not everything is constructive" (1 Cor. 10:23). Paul is challenging believers to prayerfully think through their choices in life.

But giving people the freedom to think and interact with God in faith is a scary enterprise. There is something in us that compels us to want assurance that people are "getting" exactly what God is saying— so we kind of add stuff to the truth.

KIDS AND COLOR

Think about raising children. Either you can give them your conclusions, or you can give them raw data (the kind communicated to us in Scripture) and allow them the freedom to think and disagree and argue various positions with you. If you do that, you will probably be up many nights with bazillions of colorful conversations—some of them bordering on shouting matches. However, if you include your kids in the process of considering truth and finding its application, you will discover that they are often far more conservative than you. It just doesn't pay for a parent to take a repressive and prohibitive stance. More often than not, kids in those environments run from their parents and from God.

People who speak in absolutes are generally just trying to protect people from potentially harmful activities. But if we don't trust people and invite them to participate in arriving at conclusions, *are we really helping them?*

Some people think, "If you give people too much freedom, you are giving them a license to sin." I disagree. It has been my experience in more than three decades of pastoring that the people who do sinful things, who are excessive in their lifestyle, don't need a license to sin—they just sin. But if we work with people and allow them to think on more than a superficial level—giving them the raw texts and

181

philosophy of Scripture—they discover the wisdom of holiness, which will actually serve to curb the excuses people use to sin.

TWO MILES OF DITCHES

Life has so many outright gnarly issues to tackle. Consider the issue of moderation. Moderation is a touchy thing for me. I find it hard. I find it much easier to be extreme. It's easier for me to fast than to eat in moderation. And talking? I make my living jawing. I talk a lot. It's much easier to go silent than to talk with moderation, listening some, talking some. For every mile of road, there are two miles of ditches. Staying in the middle of the road—living life in moderation—seems much harder for me than hanging in the ditches of extremes.

Let's go back to the issue of drinking. This is a stickier topic than dancing, and arguably more dangerous. *To drink, or not to drink?* That is the question. The answer is simple if you are part of a community that forbids drinking. If God has called you there, just humble yourself to the rule of that community. Easy.

However, if you are trying to answer the question *from the Bible*, the task is much more daunting. This is one area where your understanding and view are dramatically influenced by your experience. If you came from a family poisoned by alcoholism, chances are that a verse like "Wine is the venom of serpents, the deadly poison of cobras" (Deut. 32:33) will resonate deeply. You probably carry a deep inner conviction that total abstinence from *all* alcoholic beverages is the Christian way to go.

However, there are many Christians who have a completely different view. They believe alcohol in moderation is perfectly acceptable (and have Bible verses to back them up). A much more complex position to manage.

A complete-abstinence view is pretty hard to defend using the

Bible. For example, what do you do with Paul's injunction to Timothy to "stop drinking only water, and use a little wine" (1 Tim. 5:23)? The arguments from the abstinence crowd begin with the claim that the wine was just grape juice. But one has to wonder how Timothy could get hold of grape juice in a culture in which Welch's processing and refrigeration had not yet been invented. Fresh grape juice would have begun fermenting in a matter of a few hours, making it inaccessible to most in the ancient world. Not to mention the lack of logic behind Paul's command to not be "drunk on wine" (Eph. 5:18) if he really meant grape juice.

Another argument goes that Paul only told Timothy to drink wine because the water was unsafe. Whether the water was unsafe or not is irrelevant to the fact that Paul told him to drink *wine*. He could have told him to drink milk or pomegranate juice.

I am certainly not condoning drunkenness here. And *that* is precisely what the biblical warning concerning alcohol is all about—it must not be consumed in *excess*. That's the other ditch. But the Bible does not say alcohol is evil.

The psalmist reflected on God's kindness, which brought "wine that gladdens the heart of man, oil to make his face shine, and bread that sustains his heart" (Ps. 104:15). The verses that warn about excessive usage should be heeded, but not used to impose a fabricated abstinence not present in the Scripture.

Warnings about excess are given in regard to food as well as alcohol. Don't be a glutton (Prov. 23:2). Don't overeat. But no one would suggest we *stop eating* because some eat too much. Similar warnings are given about money and sex and power. These things are dangerous if not approached circumspectly. But is total abstinence the solution for areas that pose the danger of excess? One of the fruits of the Spirit is self-control. What if we focused on helping disciples achieve moderation through self-control, rather than banning areas where excess is possible? But that would be messier to manage. Too colorful, perhaps.

The danger is always present that some will mess up and do things in excess. They may dance too provocatively. They may drink too much alcohol. I have found that some people *need* to completely abstain from certain things, because they are major stumbling blocks for them—everything from alcohol to ice cream.

We must be honest with ourselves. We must honestly admit if we are too immature or lack self-control to navigate with moderation in a particular area of our lives. Abstaining may be necessary for us, but we shouldn't make everyone else pay for *our* weakness.

If you have to eat the whole pie because you cannot stop after having one piece, don't put that off on others. Folks around you should be able to enjoy a piece of pie now and again without you freaking out on them. If you were a drunk and can't just have a glass of wine without chugging the whole bottle, or one beer without downing the keg, don't put that off on others either. No one should participate in drunkenness, but everyone should have the right to enjoy a glass of wine or an occasional "cold one." I think Paul's command that "each one should carry his own load" fits well here (Gal. 6:5).

Some may remember Paul's statement about not eating anything to offend a brother in Christ or cause him to stumble (1 Cor. 8:13). I certainly agree with that. However, I think one can avoid that danger by simply asking fellow believers if drinking or dancing or *whatever* is a problem for them. If they say, yes, then abstain in their presence because of your Christian love. But be careful of those who manipulate with this. Folks need to own their stuff.

"COLORPHOBIA"

We haven't even mentioned difficult topics like the roles of men and women, appropriate attire, dating, sexuality, and child rearing. These are broad topics. Complex topics. Topics where not many conclusions are voiced in Scripture—just general parameters to ponder, wonder about, pray over, and wrestle through. More color, less black-and-white. Certainly we can tell others what we believe about various issues, but I think it is more important that we respect people and trust God to guide them into the often not-so-specific statements and general tone of Scripture. We must allow individuals the right to contextualize truth for themselves and believe that God is working in them in ways we may not be able to understand. Please don't misunderstand what I am saying—*the truth never changes*, but how it is applied within the context of each person's life does. I think we need to trust both God and people more. That will mean we need to be tolerant with a little more diversity and difference of opinion—color.

Color is more complex than black-and-white. It is also more interesting. We all crave more than a black-and-white, "Pleasantville" world, but color comes with danger—evil is colorful too. But the color of righteousness is amazing and much more wonderful than the color of evil. Yet if believers are hammered with the repressive black-and-white mandates of the religious, they will never know the color of righteousness. It is a sad thing when the only color we know is the color of evil.

21

elder-brother disease: who's your daddy?

There is an unspoken understanding, especially among older Christians, that it's OK to be a hellion and an extravagant sinner—as long as you are an outsider, a pagan, one who has *never* served Christ. But if you *have* served Christ and *then* you act in a way that is unbecoming or that makes the rest of us look bad, you're going down, baby. And it's going to remain on your *permanent record*. You can be "bad-to-the-bone" as a heathen outsider and be forgiven. Hey, we will probably ask you to testify from the platform about it—but not after being a connected insider. If you knew the ropes or held some official position, and *then* go prodigal, you need to kiss your acceptance good-bye.

But I don't think Jesus holds the same opinion.

GOING PRODIGAL

The thing many overlook in Jesus's story of the prodigal son is that the son held a prominent position in his father's house before he ever went nuts. He wasn't an outsider, but a connected insider. He knew the ropes. He understood the inheritance he had and the position he held. Yet, in a blaze of utter stupidity, he grabs what he can and becomes unconscionable—he goes prodigal, which means he became rash and extravagantly wasteful.

After he wasted everything he had on all the wrong things, the Bible says, "he came to his senses" (Luke 15:17). In other words, he realized what a moron he was. After thinking it through, he set off to his father's house to humble himself and to take whatever punishment the father would dole out. But an angry father didn't meet him. Instead, he was surprised by a father's boundless love and tender embrace. Jesus used the father in this story to represent His Father, God.

The prodigal story isn't a message of a pagan coming into the family of God; it is a message of a family member returning home after being completely rebellious and patently destructive. Jesus said this guy wandered into a "distant country" and ended up "feeding pigs." Being in a "distant country" symbolized being estranged from God's kingdom and from God Himself. Feeding the pigs signified that this young man had hit rock bottom. Pigs were detestable to the Jews. These minor elements of the story communicated to Jesus's listeners that this guy was a lost cause. As He was telling it, they had to presume his sin was unpardonable.

But it wasn't.

Not only was his sin pardonable, but Jesus reveals that the father was actively watching for and anticipating the deadbeat son's return. And once he sees him from a distance, the father bolts toward him and embraces and kisses him—pig-stink and all.

The message is clear: Fallen people everywhere, those of you who once did well in the faith but somehow lost your way; those leading destructive, wasteful lives in "foreign countries," estranged from the church and from God, listen: the Father wants you home. And the instant you turn toward "Father's house," you will go from being a prodigal to becoming a pilgrim. God will run to meet you and to hug and kiss you—even though you may still have the smell and grime of swine on you.

But there is another side to the prodigal story, a much darker side. It has to do with the elder brother. The prodigal's elder brother was not excited about his younger brother's return. In fact, he was mad about it. Jesus said he "refused" to take part in celebrating his brother's return and argued that his father was being too lenient.

THEY ARE EVERYWHERE

There are "elder brothers" all over the church. These guys and gals are the ones who, like the elder brother in the prodigal story, are disciplined, diligent, and all-around model saints. They wouldn't dare demand anything from the Father. But, also like the elder brother, they have an agenda: performance. That's what they believe the economy of the kingdom of God is all about. They work to earn God's blessing and are quick to jump on anyone who might be trying to secure blessing *without* working for it. They have elder-brother disease.

Though the elder brother refused to ask for his inheritance, he kept working hard—and cross-fingered—hoping to get the father to notice and reward him. When he sees his father celebrating the "washout" with a fatted calf and a party, he is angered. He says to the father, "Look! All these years I've been slaving for you and never disobeyed your orders. Yet you never gave me even a young goat so I could celebrate with my friends. But when this son of yours who has squandered your property with prostitutes comes home, you kill the fattened calf for him!" (Luke 15:29–30).

The elder brother completely misunderstood how things work in Father's house. The father responds, "My son, you are always with me, and everything I have is yours." The truth was, the elder brother never had to "slave" to earn what was in his father's house—everything there *already* belonged to him. His "right" to the goods of Father's house was based on the father's love, not on the son's performance. It, too, was grace.

When those of us who are older in Christ see the failure of others and God's unwarranted and incautious restoration of them, His kindness, forgiveness, and love often seem irrational and even unfair. We don't understand the Father. How different this story would have read if the prodigal had run into the elder brother first. I am certain he would have turned back to the pigs.

I have witnessed folks being written off by the elder brothers. And for good reason—the prodigals acted improperly and hurt their fellow believers. And now they are labeled. Labels are always paralyzing.

Has anyone ever labeled you a "misfit" or "rebellious" or "inconsistent" or "untrustworthy"? If so, you probably agree that it wouldn't be so bad if the labels were said to your face and the accuser actually commited to helping you work through your stuff. But more often than not, the labels are a kind of insulation between you and others. They are reminiscent of the "kick me" signs people used to stick on your back without your knowledge in grade school. People may be courteous to your face, but you can see it in their eyes: something's up. And when you walk away, you know you have about as much a chance of belonging as a snowball in hell. It's easy to think about going back to the pigs under such conditions. At least pigs don't reject you.

LIVING ON WELFARE

There is something in us that wants to earn rights from God.

The elder brother thought he could earn favor. He thought his hard labor and faithfulness were securing a place in the father's eyes. He angered when he discovered his efforts were *not* the basis for the father's kindness and gifts. Elder brothers have a hard time with this; they want to earn their keep. They don't want to be on welfare.

Years ago I was between jobs and had no income. Someone told me I qualified for unemployment and should apply. But something in me resisted. I didn't want to go down to the unemployment office, stand in line in front of a bunch of other people, and ask for a check for work I had not done. The reason? I was too proud.

I imagine if things got bad enough, I could work through my pride, but the fact still remains, I don't like charity—if *I* am the recipient. I like to show charity to others, though. Jesus said, "It is more blessed to give than to receive" (Acts 20:35). If for no other reason, that's because you *have it* to give. It is awful to be helpless and in need of someone else's strength. That's why we don't like being on the receiving end of charity.

But that is exactly how a relationship with God works. We are total charity cases. Paul claimed, "For from him and through him and to him are all things. To him be the glory forever!" (Rom. 11:36). Salvation, the kingdom of God, Christianity—these things are not initiated by us; they are the stuff of God.

ARISTOTLE VERSUS JESUS

The Greek culture surrounded the lives of Jesus and the early disciples. Though the Jews were a distinct culture within the larger Greek culture, Greek thought heavily influenced them. Even the New Testament was written in Greek. And just as we moderns feel the pressure to conform to the values and mores of our culture, the early disciples experienced that too.

Much of the Greek worldview was rooted in the teachings of the ancient philosopher, Aristotle. Aristotle was brilliant. His approach to logic and reasoning still impacts the world of thought today.

elder-brother disease: who's your daddy?

In the first four centuries of her existence, as the Church was trying to formulate her beliefs about who God was, who Jesus was, who the Holy Spirit was, how salvation is realized, how the church was to be organized, etc., the early church fathers leaned heavily on logic and formulas developed by Aristotle in order to arrive at a theology that was comprehensive and consistent.

Though the Church considered the revealed truth in the writings of the apostles and prophets sacrosanct, they believed God also revealed Himself in other ways. They had no problem drawing from Greek thought, as long as it did not violate the Scriptures.

What does this have to do with the elder brother? I'm suggesting that the elder brother based his righteousness, or the reason he had the "right" to be in Father's house and to experience the blessings of Father's house, on the footing of thoughts espoused by Aristotle, not thoughts espoused by grace—the gospel. Understanding this will shed light on the elder brother's contempt for the prodigal.

Let me explain.

For Aristotle, a person became good or right if he or she had consistently chosen right activity. Aristotle believed goodness or virtue could only be secured by human action—it is not done *to* you; it is secured by a perfection or "flowering" of one's humanity. Aristotle held that everyone must discover his or her function, or *ergon*. Once one does, that individual is well formed and worthy of promotion. The ergon of a hammer is to drive nails. The function of a saw is to cut wood. And the function of a person is to understand excellence and to attain it via proper upbringing and training. According to Aristotle, to be a person of worth, one must demonstrate his or her ability to choose the noble and avoid the base. He or she must embrace the *proper things*.

Aristotle taught that goodness was formed by a person's inner set of habits, or *ethos*. Here is how that works: when faced with a choice, first, we deliberate; then we choose; finally, we act. As we act, what we are "made of" is realized. If we are in the *habit* of making good choices (virtue) versus being in the *habit* of making bad choices (vice), we will have righteousness—the right to be noble and exalted in the public eye.

But here is the rub: Aristotle believed that virtue (the practice of good habits) was only possible for a person who was well educated from birth. The average Joe or Jane doesn't have a chance. Anyone who has made mistakes in life doesn't have a chance. His view meant that virtue was exclusive to the elite, the superior, the aristocracy. Only the well-formed person need apply. Elder brothers agree, which is why a prodigal would be disqualified forever. The fact that the prodigal failed proved that he was never virtuous to begin with—he was always a fraud. And exposing frauds just makes the elder brothers all that more elite and superior.

The ancient world bought into Aristotle's view completely. Good, noble people were only so because of a lifelong commitment to good and noble acts. This is one of the reasons the gospel was met with such resistance in the first century. Christianity made goodness chiefly a matter of grace—not the result of embracing right habits.

The gospel came into a world that held certain virtues as hallowed. If you possessed them, you were deemed good; if you didn't, you were deemed evil, and it would be wrong to have anything to do with you.

One story in the Gospels made many pagans laugh at Christianity. It was the story about Jesus and the thief on the cross. Tradition calls that thief Saint Dismas. Dismas was dying as a criminal. He was getting what he deserved. He obviously had developed no virtue. He certainly was not worthy of any kind of honor or acceptance. Yet at the door of death, Jesus welcomes him into His kingdom. The thief has done *nothing* to deserve this. He has taken no action. And there is no time for him to do anything in the future. His future is over. He is simply accepted and deemed virtuous by divine fiat!

Many pagans found this story outlandish and completely unjust.

The same was true for the prodigal story. In the ancient world, people didn't get a second chance. If you violated public trust, it was over. The more qualified "others" (like the elder brother) would take the place you so foolishly abandoned.

Just like our modern age, the ancient world was a world of retribution. If you were good, you got good. If you were bad, you got bad. If you were beautiful, you got privilege. If you weren't, you didn't. Sustained human perfection was the only hope for good in the world. It was anything but a culture of grace.

But the gospel is not a message that calls us to human perfection; it is a message that calls us to the perfect One. Faith has merit by virtue of Someone else's act. *Solo gracia.* God's very being is activity. He is active in us. And as a result, we are beatified   declared worthy of the blessedness of heaven. We are also beautified—made beautiful, acceptable, and welcomed. It is done *to* us, not *by* us.

The gospel purports that grace isn't the result of embracing excellence through a good upbringing or adequate training. To be a good person in God's kingdom, we don't have to demonstrate our ability to choose the noble over the base. In fact, to qualify as a virtuous person in Christianity, *we don't have to develop at all.* We just join to the One who *is* virtuous—Jesus Christ—and we are accepted; we belong; we're worthy. There are no entrance standards—beggars are welcome; anyone illiterate, ill-bred, or untrained fits in; criminals are accepted; betrayers are received—and good men and women are welcome—all on the same basis, all equal.

WHAT ABOUT VIRTUE?

Doesn't God expect us to live virtuous lives? Absolutely! But there is a caveat. It is *how* we live virtuous lives that is the million-dollar question. Do we attain virtue by what we do or by what is done *to us?*

193

Aristotelian virtue versus divine virtue has everything to do with origins—where it comes from. Aristotelian virtue or goodness comes through herculean human effort. It's about building good habits over a lifetime.

Divine virtue or goodness, on the other hand, comes to us through simple faith. On some metaphysical level, we participate in God's goodness, the divine nature (2 Peter 1:4). And there is transformation. Paul describes the effect of the commingling of the Divine with the human heart: "He brings gifts into our lives, much the same way that fruit appears in an orchard—things like affection for others, exuberance about life, serenity. We develop a willingness to stick with things, a sense of compassion in the heart, and a conviction that a basic holiness permeates things and people. We find ourselves involved in loyal commitments, not needing to force our way in life, able to marshal and direct our energies wisely" (Gal. 5:22–23 MSG).

This isn't the result of our efforts; this is done *to us* by grace. The murderer, the rapist, the adulterer, the proud, the self-righteous, *anyone* can experience transformation in a moment. The fruit emerges—willingness, compassion, basic holiness, loyalty, etc., all come forth in our lives because of our connection to God, not because of our performance. We experience God's virtue, not the man-made, Aristotelian kind. When we participate in divine goodness, it transforms us from the inside out.

Aristotelian virtue may be the performing of good, but it isn't much more than that—a performance. The reality is, you can look good on the outside and still be bad on the inside. The Pharisees of Jesus' day fit in here. He said they looked beautiful and good on the outside, but inside they were "full of dead men's bones" (Matt. 23:27).

What does that mean?

Jesus explained that real goodness is not pasted on the outside while there is evil raging on the inside. Many thought they were doing God's will because they never openly disobeyed commandments—

they never murdered anyone, for example. But Jesus said if you have anger in your heart (which, unchecked, could eventually lead to murder), the judgment is the same (Matt. 5:22). Basically, you are *already* a murderer in God's eyes. He said you might not openly commit adultery, but if you entertain lustful thoughts (which could end in adultery), you are already an adulterer (v. 28). Jesus was saying that you are in sin whether you *actually* do the evil thing, or just *want to* do it.

This means that whether you're a profligate sinner in prison, who has murdered and committed adultery, or a teaching Pharisee conducting a study in the Pentateuch, with anger and lust in your heart, you are the same in God's eyes.

Here is the point: there is no way to change the heart with human effort. It is hopelessly wicked. That is why God is disinterested in Aristotelian virtue. It may make you look good on the outside, but you stay the same on the inside.

WORMS AND MEN

Several years ago I was jogging in my neighborhood and ran across a large earthworm writhing on the hot pavement. He had been washed onto it from an early morning rain and was doing all he could to find earth again, but to no avail. All his energetic struggling was meaningless. He was stuck on the burning concrete and was losing against the hot noonday sun. After I ran past him, the thought came: *Go back and save that worm.* My first reaction was, *Gross!* But I went back, picked him up, and placed him in a damp, muddy drainage area. I remember leaving the scene thinking, *That's exactly what God did for me. I was hopelessly stuck in the wrong place. No matter how hard I wiggled and writhed and expended energy, it was meaningless. I needed to be picked up by someone bigger than me and set into a place of safety.*

Aristotelian discipline, which is really motivated by a longing for political power or some other perceived benefit, cannot secure true internal transformation and holiness. No matter how hard we try to choose the noble and avoid the base, whether we habitually make good choices over bad ones, we will never be righteous—not deep inside.

The elder brother got angry because the prodigal, who had squandered his money living wildly, ended up getting back what he had wasted. It wasn't fair. You almost get the impression that the elder brother is saying, "I disciplined myself, while he went out and had fun. Who wouldn't like to live wildly? But I didn't. I *disciplined* myself. And for what? I didn't get what I was after anyway, and it all went to him. What good does it do to live right?"

A friend of mine was telling me about a minister who had a moral failure but had been restored and was doing quite well. As my friend was discussing the situation with another minister, this man replied (to my friend's horror), "I think it's terrible that he is back in ministry. Who wouldn't want to commit adultery? The only reason I haven't is because I value my ministry."

Think about that. The minister's motive for not sinning was purely external. This isn't transformation. Transformation only occurs when we are in direct connection with the divine nature. When that occurs, we transcend sin—it no longer has dominion over us. Our mind is clear and clean.

Jesus told His disciples, "For I tell you that unless your righteousness surpasses that of the Pharisees and the teachers of the law, you will certainly not enter the kingdom of heaven" (Matt. 5:20). In this context Jesus was talking about not having anger or lust in your heart. When God connects with the human life, there is transformation. You don't commit murder, and you no longer hate. You don't commit adultery or have lust in your heart. You do right. But this kind of righteousness is the result of the God–man connection, not Aristotelian effort.

The key is not to fight for the flowering of human potential, but to stay connected to God. Christ following is not about how well we perform by developing Aristotelian virtue; it's about how well we cling to Jesus. Faith is not our responsibility; it's our response to God's ability.

God hates Aristotelian virtue or goodness. When a person is prodigal, at least she knows she needs virtue. Those filled with Aristotelian virtue don't feel they need God. They set aside God's goodness by seeking to establish their own. Paul claimed that this was the problem with most of the Jews—they ignored "the righteousness that comes from God and sought to establish their own," and "they did not submit to God's righteousness" (Rom. 10:3).

The truth is, people are closer to evil and damnation with Aristotelian virtue than they are as prodigals. That is why Jesus said the kingdom is close to "the poor in spirit" and "those who mourn" and "the meek" and "those who hunger and thirst for righteousness" (Matt. 5:3–6). Paul said it belongs to "the foolish" and "the weak" and "the lowly" and "the despised" (1 Cor. 1:27–28). Pagan Aristotle would never have agreed; neither does the elder brother.

THE DECHURCHED

There are millions of failed believers still in the pigpen because the elder brothers have positioned themselves at the doorposts of the church. These self-righteous boys and girls are keeping prodigals away. The protective, performance-based view of the elder brother is a spiritual disease, and it is the biggest cause of the "dechurched" of America—those who still love God but hate church.

Let me leave you with a scary thought: the elder brother still runs most religious organizations and institutions. Perhaps that is why most organized churches are losing their voice in our culture.

22

politicitus: is God a republican?

Something in me wants to believe God is a Republican. I'm a Republican. I like the idea of smaller government and less taxes, and I think the abortion and gay-rights agendas have gained too much ground. However, I suspect that my political preferences may have been fashioned more by my upper-middle-class upbringing than by what I have read in the Bible.

Some years ago I was preaching in a large charismatic church in St. Louis, Missouri—right after President Clinton and the Democrats won the White House. As were all good Republicans, I was depressed and downcast. And, like most evangelicals, I presumed God was as well. In my message that Sunday morning, I lamented the loss of the election and decried the legacy of abortion and gay rights that were sure to gain greater footing in our culture under the Democratic watch.

Immediately after the service, a very handsome, astute couple approached me. The woman spoke up: "Pastor Gungor," she said, "I have always enjoyed and appreciated your ministry here, but this morning I am afraid you have offended me."

"I'm sorry," I replied. "What exactly did I do?"

"Have you ever had a son or daughter or a niece or nephew murdered in a drive-by shooting?"

"No," I responded, a little puzzled.

"How would you like to tuck your daughter in an iron bathtub on Saturday nights just to protect her from that sort of thing?"

"I wouldn't like that," I replied sheepishly.

"Do the majority of young boys in your neighborhood get strung out on drugs or get into gangs?" she asked further.

"No," I answered, realizing where she was going.

"I certainly agree with you that God is against abortion and homosexuality, but are those the *only* sins God is concerned with? Are you suggesting that God doesn't care about the murders of innocent children through drive-by shootings in the inner city or the destruction of young lives through gangs and drugs? Are those sins of *less* concern to God, or do you suppose they are just of less concern to folks like you, who have been insulated and isolated from the concerns that befall those of us in the urban jungle?"

I knew the questions were rhetorical and her tone passionate, so I just humbly continued to listen.

"The Democratic Party may not resolve the issues that plague the inner city," she continued, "but at least they are willing to talk about them and listen to those of us who do care. Because of that, we certainly don't share the view that the victory of the Democratic Party was, in any way, a loss for the kingdom of God. And we don't feel it was appropriate for you to suggest that people of faith should feel the way you do."

I was stunned. I apologized and walked away, embarrassed that I did not have the crimes that ravage the inner city on my ethical or moral radar screen—embarrassed that I suffered from "politicitus." What if I lived in a neighborhood ravaged by drugs and violence? What if my own daughter had to sleep in a bathtub at night? Would I be as offended by gay rights or abortion advocates? Would I vote differently?

At that moment my tendency to categorize some sins as worse than others was abandoned. It was James who said, "For whoever obeys the whole of God's law and yet stumbles at just one point is

199

guilty, period. For the one who said, 'Do not commit adultery,' is also the one who said, 'Do not murder.' If you break one rule, you break them all" (James 2:10–11, author's paraphrase). In other words, sin is sin. There are no "worse" ones that God wants us to pour all our efforts into stopping. Homosexuality and abortion are not more heinous in God's eyes than murder or robbery in the inner city.

I am still a Republican, and I vote Republican. I honestly believe that the most long-term benefit to America will be garnered by the philosophy espoused by the Republican agenda. However, today I am more sympathetic to those of a contrary position. And in all honesty, neither party is completely right. For example, the Democratic solution to poverty seems to focus more on immediate, right-now help. But Republicans argue that right-now help creates problems—it overburdens the taxpayers and creates a crippling dependency. I personally agree more with the Republican solution to poverty: education. Education encourages independence and responsibility. Over the long haul, a good education will empower people to secure a better life. But tell that to a poor inner-city first-grader who is going to bed hungry tonight because her single parent has lost her job! This child will not be all that excited about the Republican solution. I'm not sure the parent will be either.

Bottom line is, at this point in my life, I am not nearly as prone to homogenize my evangelical faith with my political party affiliation. Nor am I so quick to judge those who vote Democratic. I don't assume that they are pro-gay and pro-choice, any more than I want them to assume I am greedy and uncompassionate just because some Republicans have a reputation for being that way.

Perhaps we should all just vote our convictions and leave the results in the hands of God. Maybe we should dare to believe that "the Most High is sovereign over the kingdoms of men and gives them to anyone he wishes" (Dan. 4:17).

Happy voting.

23

evangelistic rabies:
less biting, more listening

I have more questions than answers about how we evangelicals ought to approach evangelism. I'm not sure we have it all right. I'm not saying we need less intensity, I think we need *more*—a little more understanding about exactly *what* evangelism is, a little more clarity in our message, a lot more kindness and humility.

But many of us Christians are more rabid and biting than loving and engaging. Often, we communicate like people building a multi-level business—using and pressuring people—rather than imitating the apostle Paul and giving others "not only the gospel of God but our lives as well" (1 Thess. 2:8).

Sometimes I wonder if we are missing the *main* point. Many think the main point of the gospel is simply to *believe* something. That's all. If that's true, then God's dream is fulfilled when we believe that He sent Jesus to die for our sins. Once we accept that, *bingo!*—we're saved. It's all kind of anticlimactic from there. After we hit *bingo*, we just busy ourselves with responsibilities and do-gooding until we die or Jesus comes back.

But what if the gospel is more than a first-class ticket to eternity in the heavenlies? It certainly includes salvation, but what if the central point of the gospel is something more than that? What if God's dream was never *just* to create people so they could believe something in order to prepare them for a place called heaven?

THE GOAL OF EVANGELISM

We have no idea what God was thinking right before He decided to create the universe. We don't know what He was thinking when He decided to make fourteen thousand different kinds of ferns instead of just one or two. We don't know what was on His mind when He created the angels or when He made the hippo so . . . *hippo-ish*. But we do know *exactly* what He was thinking when He made the human race. It's captured in Genesis: "Then God said, 'Let us make man in our image, in our likeness, and let them rule'" (1:26).

God created the human race to be a reflection of *Himself.* He designed us to look like God, if He were flesh. We know God created us like Him so we could experience community with Him, but this text gives us insight into another reason for our likeness. We were created like Him in order to "rule" with Him.

In the creation moment, humans become reflections of God's image, His likeness. We look like Him. Then, amazingly, He sends us into His world to rule for Him, to represent Him. The Latin phrase for "the image of God" is *imago dei*. God was thinking, *I want my* imago dei *present in the earth.*

Here is what God *wasn't* thinking: "Let's create some beings who can believe a story we make up, accept it, go to church on Sunday mornings to sing and give their tithes, and listen to the Bible being taught. Then when they die, they'll get to do the good stuff—they can go to a special place called heaven, dress in white, play harps, and hang with angels, while experiencing a perpetual spiritual high."

Contrary to what many think, God isn't trying to get us to heaven. According to Scripture, eternity is spent *here*, on planet Earth. God's intent has always been to eventually come here to live in His creation. In the end, heaven actually comes to earth! (See Revelation 21.)

Yes, believers who die now go to heaven, but heaven is *not* the point. Earth is. Why is that?

As you read about the Creation event, you notice that God moved everything from chaos to order—that is the creative gesture. When God creates His first *imago dei*, Adam, He commissions him to "take care of" the Garden of Eden and to "name" the animals—to participate in moving creation from chaos to order (Gen. 2:15, 19). We weren't just created to fellowship with God; we were created to work with Him too. All of us are to be participants in the creative gesture—working to move things from chaos to order.

The reason we obey God is to release *order*, which is His kingdom, into the earth. The reason we train our kids is to bring *order*, God's kingdom, into the earth. The reason we fight to make our marriages and friendships work is because we want to bring order, or God's kingdom, into the earth. For this same reason, we participate in work that lifts and helps humanity. In eternity future, we will participate with God in bringing order to the entire universe—working for His kingdom to come and His will to be done.

The point of evangelism is more than just to get people to believe the history of Jesus. The gospel is an invitation to a new kind of living. It is the path to discovering the very purpose for which we exist—to fellowship and work with God as His *imago dei*! The reason Christ's sacrifice at the cross was necessary was because sin entered the Garden and the *imago dei* was marred.

Scripture says, "All have sinned and fall short of the glory of God" (Rom. 3:23). What does that mean? It means sin made us *less* than God intended us to be—we couldn't reflect His image anymore. The Cross fixed that. We must believe in Jesus' payment for our redemption *so we can be restored to God's original dream*. But what was that dream? His dream was always to create an *imago dei* race—a people created in His image for the express purpose of fellowship with God and participation in the work of God. God invites us to *co-rule* with Him in the fighting of chaos and the preserving of order in creation— and we will do it with Him for eternity!

We're not just going to play harps.

Evangelism is not so much a call to *believe* as it is a call to *become*. We *believe* to *become*. We preach the gospel to the marred masses in order to see them restored to the *imago dei*. Restored men and women commune with God and begin the work of moving their lives, and the lives of those within their sphere of influence, from chaos to order, from darkness to light, from the power of Satan to the power of God. Evangelism is a kingdom thing.

WHEN DOES GOD COME?

One of the things that has always confused me is trying to figure out *when* God makes himself real to a person. As an evangelical, the idea that God doesn't show up till one of us evangelicals walks into the room has been engrained in my ideology (though it was never overtly stated). We tend to be a pretty exclusive bunch. I'm sure the average evangelical would think it's silly if we stopped and thought about it, but we act as though we carry the patent on God's book and God's way—as if we have the exclusive rights to kingdom activity in the earth. If you are any other brand of Christianity, we evangelicals believe you need to talk to one of us—we are pretty certain that no generic brands lead to true salvation. We know the sinner's prayer—the right one. And since we tend to believe we are the only kingdom distributors that God has, we think you are pretty lucky if you know us.

As a child, I remember attending a movie that was sponsored by a well-known evangelistic association. At the end of the movie, a gentleman started talking at the front of the theater. I thought it was odd theater etiquette, but I stayed and listened. The guy invited people to come forward if they had questions about God.

I had questions about God. I had a deep love for Him. So I shot up front and chatted with a man who was at least 150 years old. He used language I had never heard before, like being "born again." And he seemed to have everything about faith figured out. That seemed unusual to me, even as a child.

There were no questions asked. I wasn't asked about the faith I had. I was an altar boy in my Catholic church and had a very tender place in my heart for God. But none of that seemed to matter. I was told what I needed, based on a number of Bible verses that I had never heard. I remember feeling a little offended that talked to me as though I knew nothing about God. The evangelistic terms he used were completely new to me, but loving God wasn't. But no clue was given that he believed God was anywhere near me—not as a Roman Catholic—not until *he* showed up.

There is a very provocative story in the book of Acts about the apostle Paul's visit to the pagan city of Athens. Christ had never been preached there, and Paul was amazed at how religious the city was. It was full of idols and idol worship.

At first the Bible says Paul was "greatly distressed" (17:16). But as he walked around, you get the feeling he was looking for some-thing—it appears that he was looking for evidence of God's king-dom in their midst. He ends up claiming that they were "very religious" because God was *already* at work in their culture. He points to an altar, which has been built to an "Unknown God" and says, "I'm here to introduce you to this God so you can worship intelligently, know who you're dealing with" (v. 23 MSG).

He tells the Athenians that God has always been with them, that He had even "determined the times set for them and the exact places where they should live." Think of that. God destined them to be in Athens—though it was not a Christian city. And He had done this so people "would seek him" and "find him" because He was "not far from each one of [them]." He even claimed that all people are wrapped in God's care—that "in him we live and move and have our being."

205

This story is stunning to me. Paul was saying that God was present and working in that pagan culture *before* he got there with the gospel! The gospel was simply the clearest way to reveal what God was up to. It reveals to people how God wants them to cooperate with Him. But whether people see what is going on or not, God still works in the life of every person, in every nation, at every moment. Most just don't know it, and they build altars to what they don't understand. It is in this context, the belief that God is always reaching out to every person, that Paul tells those in Athens that God commands "all people everywhere to repent."

What if the primary motive for the gospel is to help people "get" or "catch" the activity of God that is *already happening* in their midst—which becomes the fodder for salvation? What if God is really is working in every person, everywhere in the world? What if the gospel was a kind of "decoder ring" used to help people interpret and appropriately respond to the working of God in their lives? The appropriate response would be repentance and surrender to the lordship of Jesus Christ.

The Athenians were trying to respond to this "work of God" by building a false altar. What if the people of this age are doing the same thing? What if the building of fake altars looks like false religions and philosophies? But what if God is still *there*, working?

How would you approach the message of God differently if you thought this way, versus thinking God is nowhere except where we distribute Him through our concept of ministry? How would we talk with our wayward children or relatives or Muslim neighbors? How would we talk with those on the job who don't embrace Jesus? We may be "greatly distressed," as Paul was, when we survey the lives of those around us who are Christless, but are we looking for where God is working in their lives and trying to help them to see it? Maybe that is true evangelism.

PREGOSPEL GOD-FOLLOWERS

Richard Wurmbrand, author of *Tortured For Christ*, writes of a Russian officer who was a God-follower without knowing anything about Jesus:

> This man came to me. He loved God, he longed after God, but he had never seen a Bible. He never attended religious services. He had no religious education. He loved God without the slightest knowledge of him.
>
> I read to him the Sermon on the Mount and the parables of Jesus. After hearing them, he danced around the room in rapturous joy proclaiming "What a wonderful beauty! How could I live without knowing this Christ!"
>
> Then I made a mistake, I read to him the passion and crucifixion of Christ. He had not expected it and, when he heard how Christ was beaten, how he was crucified, and that in the end he died, he fell in an armchair and began to weep bitterly. He had believed in a Savior and now his Savior was dead!
>
> Then I read to him the story of the resurrection. When he heard this wonderful news, he beat his knees and swore a very dirty, but I think a very "holy" swear. This was his crude manner. He rejoiced and shouted for joy: "He is alive! He is alive!" Again he danced around the room, overwhelmed with happiness!
>
> He did not know how to pray our holy phrases. He fell on his knees together with me and his words of prayer were: "O God, what a fine chap you are! If I were you and you were me, I would *never* have forgiven you your sins. But you are really a very nice chap! I love you from all my heart!"[1]

When I read this, I couldn't help but get the feeling that God was at work in this Russian officer long before Reverend Wurmbrand ever met him. "Well," someone might ask, "was he *saved* before he understood the Savior and the gospel?" My evangelical theological tradition screams, "Absolutely not!" But I honestly don't know.

Paul deals with this riddle in Romans when he writes:

> When outsiders who have never heard of God's law follow it more or less by instinct, they confirm its truth by their obedience. They show that God's law is not something alien, imposed on us from without, but woven into the very fabric of our creation. There is something deep within them that echoes God's yes and no, right and wrong. Their response to God's yes and no will become public knowledge on the day God makes his final decision about every man and woman. The Message from God that I proclaim through Jesus Christ takes into account all these differences. (Rom. 2:14–16 MSG)

A BUDDHIST CHRISTIAN?

Tony Campolo, in his book *Speaking My Mind*, tells a story that raises this same question. He writes:

> A leading evangelist told me about an encounter he had with a non-Christian during a trip through China. While there, he visited the monastery, and as he entered the walled-in gardens of the place, he noticed one of the monks in deep meditation. At the prompting of the Spirit, he went over to talk to the man, and with his translator, he explained the story of Jesus. He opened the New Testament and showed him what the Bible taught about salvation. As he spoke, he noticed that the monk was visibly moved. Actually, there were tears in the monk's eyes. My friend, the evangelist, then said, "Won't you accept this Jesus into your heart and let him be your personal Savior?"
>
> The monk answered with surprise, "Accept him? How can I

accept him into my life when he is already there? All the time you were telling me about him, I heard his Spirit say, 'He is talking of me! He is talking of me!' I do not need to accept him. He is already in me, affirming the message of your Bible. I have known him for a long, long time."

My friend asked me, "Was this man possessed by Jesus before I ever arrived? Was he a Christian before he knew the name of Jesus? And, if I had not come with the gospel message, would God accept him on the Day of Judgment?"[2]

Questions. Uncomfortable ones, for we evangelicals.

MORE HUMILITY, LESS CONTROL

Maybe there is more mystery to evangelism than most evangelicals allow. We want to know exactly *how* and *when* someone is saved. We want to know, so we can get people saved and then move on to the next one who needs to get saved. We're practical. But what if salvation isn't as neat and predictable as we think? What if God works in a host of ways in every person's life?

Perhaps we should be less inclined to force everyone through our prefabricated, cookie-cutter salvation framework and be more open to the unique way God may be making Himself known in the life of a person. At the very least, these thoughts should make us a little less rabid and biting and a little more interested in the ones we meet—after all, God is already working in their lives *before* we show up.

I was sitting with an elderly evangelist friend of mine, who was one of the foremost leaders of the modern charismatic movement, in a shoe store. He was speaking at our church and wanted to pick up a new pair of shoes. He wandered for a few minutes; spotted the style he liked, and asked the young salesgirl if they had them in his size.

As she sat in front of him, fitting his new shoes, my preacher friend said out of the blue, "Miss, have you ever had an encounter with Jesus Christ?"

I watched embarrassment briefly cross her face. "I don't know," she said reflectively. "Not really."

Here is where I thought my friend would pull out his "Four Spiritual Laws" tract and go for the conversion.

"Well," he said in his kindly, elderly voice, "You have something to look forward to." Then he said, "I'll take these shoes."

Wait. What about the girl? My evangelical mind began to race. *What about nailing the conversion? Isn't this a compromise?* But something about it smacked of right. Something about it reeked of humility—of admitting God was bigger than a preacher. It was as if my friend believed that God had been working in the girl's life *before* we got there and would be working in her life after we left. There was mystery in it. It was a little messy. Not everything was clear. But there was life in it. Palpable life. I still wonder how long his words rang in that young girl's soul before she had her own encounter with the living God.

This kind of thinking doesn't change our message. It simply changes our sense of control. It causes us to walk into our conversations with others, thinking, *I wonder what God is doing in your life?* instead of, *Now that I am here, maybe you have a shot at God moving in your life.* So much of what evangelicals call evangelism may, in the final analysis, be more hubris than anything else.

What if we did buy into the idea that God was *already* engaging with folks before we show up? That would mean our job as followers of Jesus, as apprentices of the kingdom, would be to hunt for the activity of God in the lives of others (that would add some mystery and suspense to our faith—we'd be like spies for God!). What if our job is to help catch God in the lives of others, to point Him out, to help make Him famous? How fun would that be?

Some years ago, I got into a conversation with a physician that went "spiritual" after he found out I was a minister.

"I guess I'm an agnostic," he said. "I don't deny there is a God, but I can't say there is one either."

"I totally get that," I replied.

"Really?" he asked, a bit surprised to hear that from a minister.

"Yeah," I continued. "We are talking about believing in someone who is invisible. The whole idea of faith leaves things in the realm of 'maybe, maybe not'."

We chatted for a while about belief in general, and then I said, "Here's the cool thing, Doc: God is everywhere, working in everyone's life. People just miss Him. He's working somewhere in your life too. Faith is just about 'catching' Him, not making Him come.

"Let me ask you a question," I continued. "Was there ever a time in your life when you felt a kind of 'otherly' peace surrounding you? Like something was transcendent around you?"

"Yeah," he said. "That's why I love hiking in the mountains. I get up there, and I feel a kind of serene presence. Nature, I guess."

"That's God," I asserted. "I dare you to try something. Next time you are hiking and you feel that serenity, talk to it. Ask it, 'Are you Jesus?' If it's really Him, He will talk back—maybe not in words, but in a way that will be undeniable to you."

I gave him my address and told him to contact me if anything ever happened. About two months later, I was surprised to get a letter from him. He said he had been out mountain climbing and came to a particularly beautiful ridge. As the serenity of the scene hit him, our conversation came back to him.

"Reluctantly, I did just what you said," he wrote. "I asked, 'Are you Jesus?' After a moment, there was a response. Not words, but somehow I knew it was Him. Some kind of joy exploded in me. What do I do now?"

The guy met Jesus—but it was the same Jesus he had only

previously known as a *serene feeling* in nature. He had no idea that in those moments, God was reaching out to him. His mountain hikes were like the Athenians' altar to the "GOD NOBODY KNOWS." Maybe we gospel heralders are to say what Paul said to that bunch: "I'm here to introduce you to this God so you can worship intelligently, know who you're dealing with" (Acts 17:23 MSG).

If this is true, we need to tell the gospel bullhorn man to lose the evangelistic rabies, put down his bullhorn, stop talking *at* people, and start talking *with* them.

24

spiritual HIV:
together we stick; divided we're stuck

The better I get to know some people, the more I like my dog. That sounds mean, but it's true. I don't know why it's so easy to get hurt by others. Insecurity? A longing for fairness? A desire to be loved and appreciated? All of the above? Whatever the reason, getting hurt by others is part of the human experience.

I've never responded well to hurt. I always end up with self-pity arriving in my soul like a sentry for guard duty. And at those times, no one is going to get through my well-guarded emotional gate. I want to draw back from people. I get in a state of *ungiving*—I can't give people a smile, a conversation, my trust, my kindness, my *anything*. And that is precisely what unforgiveness is—*ungiving*. Forgiveness, on the other hand, is *forgiving*.

When Jesus taught on prayer, He said forgiveness was critical to the process and that unforgiveness robs the effectiveness of prayer and our ability to receive God's help (Mark 11:26). That stinks, because I've been in unforgiveness more times than I care to admit: when my expectations went unmet; when an unexpected betrayal was realized; when I encountered meanness, rudeness, or being overlooked by others; when people expected too much from me; and when I felt used.

It doesn't take long to fall in love with your dog.

213

Unforgiveness is a kind of HIV to the human soul. HIV (human immunodeficiency virus) is a virus that steadily weakens the body's defense, or immune, system until it can no longer fight off even simple infections. Unforgiveness does the same to the human soul. Love, kindness, mercy, justice, and the like—the immune system of human relationships—all wither when unforgiveness infects us. Unforgiveness weakens the human soul to the point that the simple stresses of everyday life become too much to bear, and the infections of anger, strife, revenge, hatred, and indifference rule.

THE TRAP

Jesus said offense always shows up in our relationships at one point or another (Matt. 18:7 KJV). All of us have experienced that. But He warns us to resist offense. Interestingly, the word Jesus uses to describe how others offend us is the Greek word *skandalon*, from which we get our English word *scandal*. Literally, *skandalon* refers to the movable stick, or "trigger," of an animal trap. Get the imagery here. You set up a trap and put in a scrap of food. The animal you are after enters the trap to snag the food. He hits the trigger, the trap door falls, and you are an official trapper.

The "trapper" in the spiritual context is the enemy of our souls, Satan. When people do hurtful things to us, Satan loves to see us run "instant replays" of the event over and over in our minds. Often thoughts inspired by Satan run through our minds with machine-gun rapidity: *Why? How did this happen? What were they thinking? Do I even matter to them?* And we begin to pace back and forth inside the event, like a caged animal. If we do not purposely try to forgive the incident, *offense* is born—*skandalon* occurs. The trigger is pulled, and the trap door falls.

We're stuck. Helpless. Powerless.

When we are trapped in offense, we stop progressing spiritually. Paul warned, "If angry, beware of sinning. Let not your irritation last until the sun goes down; and do not leave room for the Devil" (Eph. 4:26–27 WOR). Setting up a "room for the Devil" sounds like a bad idea. But that is exactly what we do when we *focus* so much on an offense that it influences the way we act.

Gail and I have gotten stuck hosting one or two very weird people in our home over the years. They made us nervous the whole time they were in our house. We didn't sleep well and were happy to see them leave. What if you had the Antichrist stay overnight? Would you sleep well? Would you worry about your kids in the next room? Well, Satan is the Antichrist's dad. Allowing the irritations of people to fester in your mind after "the sun goes down" causes unforgiveness to dawn. Unforgiveness, unresisted and unchecked, is a welcome mat for Satan to move into your home. No good can come from that.

THE CURE

So how do we resist something that comes on us like an armed man? How do we process the overwhelming feelings of offense and unforgiveness? The Greek word translated "forgiveness" is *aphieemi*, literally, "to send off," "to release," or "to let go." This suggests that forgiveness is the act of *sending away* incidents that cause offense to brew in us. We can't keep focusing on the wrong done to us.

This is how God deals with the way we offend Him. Instead of getting into unforgiveness with us over our sin, He chooses to forgive us by sending our sin away. God sends our sins "as far as the east is from the west" (Ps. 103:12). The prophet Micah wrote that God would "cast all [our] sins into the depths of the sea" (Micah 7:19 KJV).

This is the way we are to forgive one another. Paul said, "Forgiving each other, just as in Christ God has forgiven you" (Eph. 4:32). When we forgive others, we must "send away" the sins they commit against us. We cannot let the bad things others do to us linger in our minds—not if we want to walk in forgiveness.

But how do we do that? Not easy. This is at the heart of what Christians call "spiritual warfare." Satan wants us to think our struggles in life are with "flesh and blood"—against people (Eph. 6:12). But Paul claims our struggle is really with the forces of darkness—there is spiritual warfare. Darkness is seeking a place to live. It wants to overwhelm us. If we become convinced that people are the problem, and we hold sins committed against us in our minds after "the sun goes down" (or the incident passes), we "leave room for the Devil"—we invite Satan and his demonic agenda into our lives.

But there are some helpful thoughts I have found, which aid in the forgiveness process.

HELPFUL THOUGHT #1: TRY TO UNDERSTAND

I read a story a number of years ago that shows how *understanding* empowers forgiveness:

Once there was a boy who lived with his mother and grandfather. His grandfather was not really an elderly man, but he was confined to a wheelchair and had very little use of his arms. His face was badly scarred, and he had a difficult time swallowing his food.

Every day the little boy was assigned the task of going into his grandfather's room and feeding him lunch. This the little boy did faithfully, but not joyously. It was quite a mess to feed Grandfather.

As the boy grew into adolescence, he became weary of his responsibility. One day he stormed into the kitchen and announced that he had had enough. He told his mother, "From now on, you can feed Grandfather."

216

Very patiently his mother turned from her chores, motioned for her son to sit down, and said, "You are a young man now. It is time you knew the whole truth about your grandfather." She continued, "Grandfather has not always been confined to a wheelchair. In fact he used to be quite an athlete. When you were a baby, however, there was an accident."

The boy leaned forward in his chair as his mother began to cry.

She said, "There was a fire. Your father was working in the basement, and he thought you were upstairs with me. I thought he was downstairs with you. We both rushed out of the house leaving you alone upstairs. Your grandfather was visiting at the time. He was the first to realize what happened. Without a word he went back into the house, found you, wrapped you in a wet blanket, and made a mad dash through the flames. He brought you safely to your father and me.

"He was rushed to the emergency room suffering from second- and third-degree burns as well as smoke inhalation. The reason he is the way he is today is because of what he suffered the day he saved your life."

By this time the boy had tears in his eyes as well. He never knew; his grandfather never told him. And with no conscious effort on his part, his attitude changed. With no further complaints, he picked up his grandfather's lunch tray and took it to his room.[1]

Understanding puts things in perspective and helps us let things go—that's what forgiveness is.

Have you ever been misjudged by someone else? It happens all the time. For example, let's say your wife asks you to mow the lawn this afternoon. You plan to do it, but then a friend stops by that you haven't seen for a while, and you end up chatting for a couple of hours. Now there is not enough time to mow the lawn. You feel a pang of guilt, but, hey, you *intended* to mow the lawn, so in a way, you did.

But then your wife comes home. Will she judge you by your intentions or your actions? Chances are, she will think something like, *He didn't mow it. Do I have to do everything around here? He doesn't have time for us, but when one of his buddies calls for help, he has all the time in the world!*

Then you feel judged. It's unfair. Offense starts to dawn in you as well.

The truth of the matter is, we tend to judge others by their *actions*, while we judge ourselves by our *intentions*—so, we tend to be much more tolerant of ourselves. One secret to obviating offense is encouraging *understanding* and refusing to jump to conclusions. We need to learn to pause in order to understand what is really going on.

Remember that factors like personality, life experiences, stress, and maturity levels (spiritual and emotional) affect the way people act. Sometimes people come across offensively because they are reacting to pain from the hurts that they have experienced in the past, and they are just trying to protect themselves from being injured again. Wounded animals do not act predictably when you approach them; neither do emotionally wounded humans. Pausing to try to understand really helps us in the forgiving process.

When Nathan and Janice walked into my office, I was surprised to learn their marriage was close to breaking up. From the outside, they looked like a great couple. Fun. Social. But they were secretly at war with each other in their marriage. A lot of it had to do with the way they each grew up.

Nathan grew up in a home where both his parents were quiet and seldom, if ever, raised their voices. In Nathan's home, raising your voice meant you were extremely angry. Janice, on the other hand, grew up in a larger family, where you had to yell or you lost your opportunity to get the potatoes at the other end of the dinner table. The only time her family got quiet was when they were really, really mad.

When incidents that required discussion arose after Janice and Nathan married, Janice would naturally begin to raise her voice. Nathan would think, *Oh my! I'd better not say another word. She has lost her temper!*

Nathan would walk silently out of the room, thinking he was helping the situation. Then Janice would think, *Why won't he talk to me? Why is he so angry? He must hate me.*

They totally misunderstood each other. And instead of working to understand each other or learning to navigate through their differences, they bought into the lie that they were not meant to be together. After seventeen years of marriage and two great teenage kids, they cashed it all in and divorced.

HELPFUL THOUGHT #2: GET THE PLANK OUT

In discussing human relationships Jesus said to "first take the plank out of your own eye, and then you will see clearly to remove the speck from your brother's eye" (Matt. 7:5). *What does that mean?*

While I was attending Bible school, Gail and I met a great friend named Bill. The only problem was, Bill was a cheapskate—he didn't carry his own financial weight. He was always asking for something: rides home, to borrow the car, to use our phone, to eat with us, to come over to our apartment on hot summer days to keep from having to turn on his air conditioner . . . You get the picture.

At first it did not bother me. I grew up in a home where we always shared what we had with others. But over time it began to bother me that Bill never even offered to chip in with expenses he was helping to incur.

By our second year of school, it was getting old. It eventually got so bad that I couldn't even look at Bill without thinking about how he was using us. In my mind, he was no longer a friend with a problem;

219

he was a problem friend. So I began avoiding him at school and even leaving the room when he visited our apartment.

At one point I commented to Gail, "He is getting on my nerves so much that I feel like punching him!" She told me I had better deal with my feelings before I said something I would regret—so I finally made it a matter of prayer.

A few days later, as I was exiting a freeway ramp, I felt God speak to me. I heard, *You're making his splinter a plank.*

"What?" I asked, puzzled.

You're making his splinter a plank, I heard again.

Immediately I remembered the verse in Matthew, which basically states that if we want to help people, we have to "first take the plank out of [our] own eye, and then [we would] see clearly to remove the speck out of [our] brother's eye" (7:5).

I was driving with my eyes wide open, and at the same time clearly viewing a minimovie inside my head. I saw our friend Bill, who had become "the cheapskate" in my mind, with what looked like a little thorn sticking out of his eye. As I lifted my hand to the thorn, an exact duplicate appeared between my thumb and index finger. In this inner vision I saw myself taking the duplicate splinter and bringing it so close to my face that all I saw was the splinter—it became so large that it had become a plank!

Lift up a finger about a foot from your face and you see your finger *and* a lot of other things. But when you bring that finger an inch from your eye, all you see is the finger—it becomes a plank. I think God was trying to show me that I had lost sight of the fact that Bill was a precious friend with a problem (or a splinter). Instead, in my eyes, he had actually become the problem (a log).

The next day when I saw Bill, I saw him with a new set of eyes. Internally, I had stopped focusing on the problem he was displaying. He was now a precious friend in Christ *with* a problem instead of a problem brother. That is when I knew I could speak with him without judgment and without hurting him. I approached him, but before I could say a word, he said, "Ed, God began dealing with me yesterday about taking advantage of you and Gail. I need to be more responsible . . . please take this twenty dollars as a start . . . I'm really sorry."

To forgive Bill, I had to separate him from his sin—I had to get the plank out. This separation opened the door for change to come—in both of us! Forgiving and releasing Bill from his sin was God's way of bringing restoration. It also set the stage for necessary change to take place in him. What if *not* forgiving Bill had been hindering God from touching him through me? What if our unforgiveness locks God's hands in all kinds of ways in our lives and in the lives of those we love? God was gracious to show me the situation through His eyes so I could forgive. It allowed the plank to become a splinter again, and then, even the splinter was effectively removed.

HELPFUL THOUGHT #3: MAKE THE DECISION

In order to walk out of the bondage of unforgiveness, we need to make the decision to release the person who has offended us. Forgiveness is not a feeling; it is an act of the will—it's a quality decision. A quality decision is a decision from which there is no retreat. You decide to release the person from his or her guilt . . . period. You may remember the offense repeatedly at first. That's OK. The commitment to forgive a person is a commitment to "send away" the incident every time it reappears in your mind.

Once the apostle Peter asked Jesus, "'Lord, how oft shall my brother sin against me, and I forgive him? till seven times? Jesus saith unto him, I say not unto thee, Until seven times; but, Until seventy times seven" (Matt. 18:21–22 KJV).

That makes 490 times.

Luke, in his gospel, adds the phrase "a day" (17:4 NASB). Imagine forgiving the same person 490 times *a day*! I call it the 490 Principle.

Some years ago one of my sisters did something that really hurt me. She was totally unaware of what she did, but the offense consumed me. I'd think about it five, even ten, times a day, and all the anger and bitterness of my soul came out against her. Then I started practicing the 490 Principle of Forgiveness and decided that every time I thought about what she did, I would prayerfully give it to God. "I give this to you, Jesus."

My thought was, *If the Cross is good enough to cover the sins I did toward God, it has to be good enough to cover sins committed toward me.* I decided it didn't matter if she ever asked for forgiveness. What Jesus did satisfied my longing for justice as far as I was concerned. And every time it came up, I thought, *490 times*—and I would forgive. After a few months, it came up only a couple times a week, and then maybe once a month. Today, I can't even remember the last time I thought about it. It's marvelous and liberating to forgive.

The choice to forgive means we *keep* forgiving—sending the sin away—every time the memory of the incident arises. You will find the incident losing strength, and you will discover new victory in God. Keep in mind that this is the same way you must forgive yourself!

HELPFUL THOUGHT #4: START GIVING

Remember, forgiveness is *forgiving*. Here are some practical ways you can give to others after an offense.

Give them your prayers. Start by praying for the one who has offended you. Jesus said, "But I tell you who hear me: Love your enemies . . . pray for those who mistreat you" (Luke 6:27–28). We are not to complain to God for the way we have been treated; we are to pray for our offender to be blessed and ask God to help us see *as He does*!

Prayer always breeds intimacy. If you pray for an enemy, he or she won't be your enemy long—God will cause you to see something good in that individual, and you will come to actually appreciate him or her.

Give them acts of kindness. These might include things as simple as a smile, a conversation, a card of appreciation, a visit, or a gift. If you will practice this, it will prepare your attitude so that your giving is done with a joyful heart. Ask the Holy Spirit to guide you.

Give them an opportunity to restore trust. When someone fails you, there is a temptation to write him off and never trust him again. That is not God's way. However, there is danger when you restore trust too quickly.

We are not commanded to trust people blindly. Trust is something that is earned, not freely given. Concerning those who influence us, the Bible warns, "They must first be tested; and then . . . let them serve" (1 Tim. 3:10). Our gift to people is the *capacity* for trust. We don't trust blindly, but we should give people the opportunity to prove themselves without being too suspicious.

Let's say that a husband gets involved in an adulterous situation. Should he ever be trusted again? The answer is yes. But, unlike the other aspects of forgiveness, trusting someone who has violated a trust should be done with some reservation—in a trust-test-trust fashion—until the person proves trustworthy again.

The principle of trust is, you meet a person, you trust him to a degree; and if he proves faithful, your trust grows. If someone has gone through this process, gaining your full trust, and then later violates it, he or she must be made to go through the process again.

Unforgiveness, however, just writes people off and does not allow them to go through the process again, once there has been offense. That is not right. Forgiveness, on the other hand, allows another chance. Still, forgiveness does not and should not ever bypass the process of rebuilding trust. That would be foolishness.

Going back to our question of, should the wife of an adulterer trust him again? The answer was yes—with qualification.

How should a wife approach this? (These next steps are the same for a forgiving husband too.) She shouldn't have to concern herself with worrying and wondering if he is up to something. But she should have the freedom to *question* him. If he comes home later than usual after work, she should ask him what happened. A simple explanation should be accepted; asking for an explanation is not to be an *interrogation*.

It is not wrong for the wife to want to know where her husband can be reached and to expect him to call when he is late. He shouldn't get away with crying, "You don't trust me." She did once, and he violated that trust. But she *should* remain open to his earning that trust again because of forgiveness—but not without his proving himself.

When Jesus was dealing with people, the Bible says, "But Jesus, on His part, was not entrusting Himself to them, for He knew all men" (John 2:24 NASB). We don't have the luxury of *knowing* all men, but we do have the biblical precedent to *test* them (1 Tim. 3:10). Trust must be earned!

Forgiveness always releases a person from the act of offense, whether he or she is sorry or not. However, *trust* is predicated upon a repentant heart and should only be given as many times as the person is truly repentant.

Confront them. "If a brother sins against you, go to him privately and confront him with his fault" (Matt. 18:15 TLB). When there has been conflict, there usually must be some direct confrontation.

When a person commits action sins against you, like stealing, sowing discord and lies, or adultery, you *must* talk with him or her about it. Many folks wrongly steer away from confrontation, and it ends up being destructive in their relationships.

Bill Hybels writes:

Tenderhearted people will go to unbelievable lengths to avoid any kind of turmoil, unrest or upheaval in a relationship. If there's a little tension in the marriage and one partner asks the other, "What's wrong?" the tender one will answer, "Nothing." What he or she is really saying is this: "Something's wrong, but I don't want to make a scene." In choosing peace keeping over truth telling, these people think they are being noble, but in reality they are making a bad choice. Whatever caused the tension will come back. The peace will get harder and harder to keep. A spirit of disappointment will start to flow through the peace keeper's veins, leading first to anger, then to bitterness and finally to hatred. Relationships can die while everything looks peaceful on the surface!

Peace at any price is a form of deception from the pit of hell. When you know you need to tell the truth, the evil one whispers in your ear, "Don't do it. He won't listen. She won't take it. It will make things worse. It's not worth it." If you believe those lies, there is a high probability that you will kill your relationship sooner or later.[2]

One of the best ways to love someone is to act in his best interests. That often means you must leave the comfort level of the relationship to deal with something that will be in the best interest of the other person. That is not easy to do. Confronting people is often very frightening.

However, there are times, when people do and say things inadvertently, that they do not need to be confronted. Often, confronting a person is more of a temptation than wisdom. We are tempted to tell people how they hurt us to somehow "get back" at them or make them feel badly.

Confrontation is not wisdom when we are not in the appropriate position to confront the person. A man confronting another man's wife on her attire; a parishioner approaching a visiting minister to correct his theology; unwanted correction of someone else's child, all are examples of inappropriate confrontation.

Sometimes, in an attempt to secure their own forgiveness, people feel they must confess their sins to the one they have sinned against. If it is an action sin, like those mentioned above, where they have violated a trust or need to give restitution, then they should do it. But if the other person has not really been affected, confrontation isn't advised.

I have been approached numerous times over the past thirty-five years by people who confessed they had a problem with me. The story usually goes something like this:

"Brother Ed, please forgive me!"

"For what?" I ask.

"Well, I have had a real problem with you over the past six months, and yesterday I finally got it resolved."

"What did I do?" I query, sort of bewildered, feeling my emotional guard going up.

"Oh, never mind. I'm free now!"

The problem is, I'm *not*. I race through my dealings with this person. *What have I done?* I ask myself. There have been times when I was tortured for days, trying to figure out what I had done to offend a person.

Confronting someone about your personal struggles with him is not wisdom and may, in fact, end up negatively impacting his life.

Dr. Charles Stanley wrote, "Confessing our forgiveness to someone who has not first solicited our forgiveness usually causes more problems than it solves. I will never forget the young man in our church who asked one of the women on our staff to forgive him for lusting after her. She had no idea he had a problem with lust, and his confession caused her to be embarrassed and self-conscious around him from then on."[3]

When giving the gift of confrontation, make sure it isn't a bomb you are delivering. Wrap it with wisdom.

CONFRONTATION

So, *how should you confront someone?* Before you actually sit down to confront a person, make sure you deal with yourself first. Start by *clarifying the issue.* Is it really something that is important, or are you just being touchy or picky? Is it something that will resolve itself after the person gains more experience, or is it a permanent issue that pervades the way the person lives? If you feel you must deal with it, what do you feel is the real root of the problem?

Second, *surrender to God.* Paul writes, "Brothers, if someone is caught in a sin, you who are spiritual should restore him gently. But watch yourself, or you also may be tempted" (Gal. 6:1). We must watch ourselves so that we do not succumb to the temptation to jump on others in a judging or criticizing fashion instead of employing *gentleness,* as this verse commands. If you feel angry or restless and you want to deal with the issue immediately, be watchful—you can hurt as easily as help people in this arena. Surrender your heart to God first. Tell Him you will sit tight until you sense His grace for wisdom, peace, and kindness within you.

Thirdly, *pray about the time and place* for the confrontation. It is important to find the appropriate time and place to share the "seeds" of confrontation. The Bible says there is "a time to plant" and a time not to (Eccl. 3:2). Just as a farmer waits for the right season to plant, as well as the best *place* for the seed, we must be sensitive to time and place.

A farmer would never run out to the field to plant during a tornado or violent thunderstorm. Don't try to plant new ideas or perspectives that you feel are important during emotional tornados and thunderstorms.

When your husband comes home for the day and his mind is still reeling from issues at work, don't try to confront him. While your wife is cooking or dealing with the children, the only input she is open to is you rolling your sleeves up and helping out. Don't try to confront her there. Late at night, when you are both tired, is not a good time either.

The conditions of time and place can make or break a confrontation situation. Set aside a special time and a quiet place to be together: a favorite restaurant, at home before the kids arrive from, on a walk, etc.

As an employer, I often have to confront those who work for me. Time and place are paramount issues to me. I try to go to someone when he is not under excessive work or personal pressure, and in a place where he feels the most comfortable. Seldom do I ask someone to "step into my office." Generally I will confront an individual in an "Oh, by the way . . ." fashion as we are walking along, or I will step into *his* office and sit in front of *his* desk. The time-and-place secret is key to effective confrontation.

Dealing with yourself and selecting the right time and place for confronting a person is a big part of the battle. You win the rest of it when you approach the person with honesty, care, and vulnerability.

THE CONVERSATION

Start your conversation by *affirming your commitment to the relationship.* Everyone is listening for the "bottom line." What is it that you want? Are you threatening them with an ultimatum? By affirming your commitment, it helps them to see that you are interested in resolving a problem, not in getting your own way in a situation.

Tell your spouse how much you love and need him or her and that your marriage is the most important thing in the world to you. Tell your boss that you appreciate the opportunity to work with him or her, or a fellow employee that you enjoy being on the same team. Tell friends that you really value their friendship.

Next, *carefully state the issue without placing blame on anyone.* Avoid broad-brushed statements like "You always . . ." or "You never . . ." The moment you say something like that, the other person's defense mechanisms turn on and he no longer hears what you are saying. It is easy to brush off such absolute statements. Stick with statements like "I feel alone" and "I feel that you are blocking me out—that I don't matter" or "It's as if nothing I say has any bearing on where we are headed. It's confusing to me." The *"I feel"* phrases will get you a lot farther than the blaming, *"you"* phrases will.

Last, *encourage and invite dialogue.* After you have gotten the issue on the table, ask, "What do you think? Am I all wet on this? Do you see any validity in what I am saying?" Honestly long for and value their perspectives. Some folks will just write you off; others will go into shock that you have confronted them; still others will open up, immediately repent, and ask you to forgive them. No matter what the result, it is always better to confront than it is to leave a relationship in a lie.

A FINAL THOUGHT

Remember that forgiveness is supernatural. You may have been tempted to say, "I can't do all this!" The truth is, you are right. Forgiveness is a supernatural act that can only be facilitated by the power of God. That is why God's choice to help us with the Holy Spirit in our relationships is so significant.

True forgiveness is not possible apart from the hand of God in your life. You may be able to partially forgive, do one or two of the steps we've described, but total unconditional forgiveness is the result of God's enablement, not human volition.

25

the hard heart: God, sex, and spirituality

So, when was the last time you felt really close to Jesus?" I asked John.

John was a Christian-radio pioneer. He was one of the first guys to put contemporary Christian music on the air. And it was a fight. He did it while pastoring full-time and raising a family of three kids.

He was sitting in my office because he was spent, and his marriage was close to being shipwrecked. I asked him about his personal relationship with Jesus. His response saddened me.

"The last time I felt close to Jesus was about fourteen years ago, right after I gave my life to Jesus."

"Didn't you feel close to Him as you grew in your faith?" I queried.

"Not really," he replied. "I was taught that since Jesus died for me, it was my responsibility to live for Him."

"How's that worked for you?" I asked.

"It hasn't," he said, head hanging. "I feel dead inside."

He was a victim of a hard heart.

HOW HEARTS HARDEN

As goes your heart, so goes your life. That's why the writer of the Proverbs warned, "Above all else, guard your heart, for it is the wellspring of life" (4:23). The *heart*, in the biblical context, is the repository of a person's deepest and sincerest feelings and beliefs, the seat of one's intellect and imagination—the deepest you.

The Scriptures describe the *heart* as God's doorway to the human life. Relationships are of the heart. When a group asked Jesus why their homes were being ravaged by divorce, He responded directly, "It was because your hearts were hard" (Mark 10:5). A relationship dies when the "heart" hardens—when the deepest part of us starts to shut down feelings and caring for another.

A heart gets hard for a whole bunch of reasons. Sometimes we get hurt in a relationship, so we harden just to protect ourselves. Other times our hearts gets cold about another because we don't pay enough attention to the other person. Jesus said whatever we "treasure" or pay attention to, our hearts will energetically follow (Matt. 6:21). No attention; no energy.

Heart hardness can happen in our relationship with God. He never gets disinterested in us, but we do Him. Do you remember when you first began your journey of faith? Remember how open and tender your heart was? Remember how God's Word, worship, and fellowship with other God-followers seemed precious to you? But as time goes on, a kind of "heart hardness" can set in. People stop seeming all that wonderful. Bible truths start to get a tad redundant—we usually grasp things after hearing them a couple of times and start to have contempt for what we hear over and over again. And just as individuals with *physical* heart problems have difficulty participating in normal life, the Christian life starts getting difficult— we tire more easily. We get hard hearts.

In a vision given to the apostle John, recorded in the book of Revelation, Jesus addresses His followers. These guys had been apprentices of Jesus for a while. And they were doing pretty good about some things. Jesus praises them for their "hard work" and "perseverance" (2:2). He applauds them for making sure false teachers weren't tolerated and people practicing wicked things were talked to. He said they had suffered "hardships" for His name and had fought and "not grown weary" (v. 3). But then He says, "Yet I hold this against you: You have forsaken your first love" (v. 4).

Obviously these guys loved God. They loved Him enough to "persevere" for Him—a devoted love. They loved Him enough to protect the integrity of His message—a rational, intellectual love. They displayed sacrificial love—a love willing to lose and accept hardship for God. They had a committed love that refused to grow "weary." But they had forsaken what He calls their "first love." And He wasn't happy. In fact, He says if they don't correct the situation, they will lose their capacity to represent Him effectively in the world; He would "remove" their "lampstand from its place" (Rev. 2:5).

What is "first love"? I would like to suggest that the kind of love Jesus is talking about is rumored in the kind of unique love shared in the marriage relationship between a husband and wife—*physical* love. This will take some explaining.

ETERNAL COPIES

Did you ever wonder how angels and devils hide from us in the seen world? And if God is everywhere, why don't we actually *see* Him? The theological answer to these questions is that there is a spiritual dimension that is different from the physical one—it is a dimension where angels, devils, and God have tangible reality. Furthermore, the Scriptures teach us that much of what we see in this world is a copy of things in the dimension of the spiritual. (That certainly lends credence to Plato's philosophical concept of *Forms*.)

Referring to the Old Testament tabernacle built by Moses, the Hebrew writer claimed that the earthly version of the temple was "just a copy" of "the real one in heaven" (Heb. 8:5 CEV). The concept of fatherhood finds its roots in God being our Father (Eph. 3:14–15). Even the idea of motherhood is anchored in God. Isaiah wrote, "Can a mother forget the infant at her breast, walk away from the baby she bore? But even if mothers forget, I'd never forget you—never" (Isa. 49:15 MSG).

Marriage also reflects something beyond itself. Paul writes, "'For this reason a man will leave his father and mother and be united to his wife, and the two will become one flesh.' This is a profound mystery—but I am talking about Christ and the church" (Eph. 5:31–32). This suggests that the marriage union, with all of its dynamic and mystery, brings insight into the relationship we are called to have with Christ. In other words, something in the relationship between a man and woman as husband and wife gives us a snapshot of what our relationship with God is supposed to be like. "Mystery" means something else is going on, beyond the obvious. This makes marriage a kind of parable. The human marriage experience is a *copy* of something eternal.

The whole marriage motif is used analogously throughout the Old and New Testaments to describe the relationship between God and man. Something about the way a man messes with a woman and a woman messes with a man gives us a glimpse into our spiritual relationship with God.

Marriage is a potpourri of loves: friendship love; devoted love; rational, intellectual love; sacrificial love; etc. But the love that is peculiar to this human bond is physical love. The Greek word for human physical love is *eros*. We get our English word *erotic* from it. *Eros* is the physical expression of the love between a husband and a wife, and there is something about it that reflects our relationship with God.

Talking about sexuality and God in the same context definitely feels uncomfortable. Perhaps the uneasiness comes from the way sexuality is abused in our culture and thereby loses its sanctity. Or perhaps it is because we have hints of ancient Gnosticism in us, which held that all physical things were evil, and comparing our spiritual relationship with Christ with the sheer physicalness of the sexual relationship seems a little out-there. But the correlation is clearly put forth in the biblical text (Song of Solomon, Pauline teaching on marriage, etc.).

THE IMPORTANCE OF *EROS*

My brother, Mark, has an organization called Laugh Your Way To A Better Marriage. He conducts marriage seminars in churches and corporations and works directly with the Pentagon to bring marriage enrichment to our troops. He helps a lot of marriages. He loves to tell stories of estranged couples who hardly sit next to each other at the start of his events and end up cuddling and holding hands by its end. He claims that physicality, touch, goo-goo eyeing, teasing whispers, and good sex are all crucial to a healthy marriage relationship.

Of course, physicality is only one dimension. There is the need for friendship, the promise of faithfulness, a demonstrated commitment, and the basic chemistry of physical attraction for carnal love to be fulfilling. But sexual love is crucial to a marriage and proves to be a kind of "cleansing" for the relationship.

A sexless marriage is a dead marriage. Why? Two reasons. First, because all the other forms of love are not unique to marriage, they are shared with others outside the marriage bond. For example, you can be friends with many people. Similarly, you can be a faithful and devoted person in general to whomever you know. Attraction isn't even unique—many different people may appear attractive to us.

Sexual love, by contrast, is exclusive to marriage—at least that was God's intent. Physical love was designed by God to be shared by one man, one woman, together, for life. To exclude carnal love from a marriage is to domesticate it, to make the relationship common—marital bonds end up looking like something one could share with a coworker or a friend.

The second reason a sexless marriage isn't a legitimate marriage is because of the "otherliness" of sex. Sexual love cannot be shared between two people unless they are both present. Fantasy can be shared separately, but fantasy isn't real. Real sexual love is shared love; it is "otherly." It demands the participation of *another*. With physical love we go out of ourselves in a trajectory of ecstasy—to a place where we cease to be in control of ourselves. We become completely vulnerable, open, engaged, and yielded to each other. In this ecstasy we lose ourselves in the "other" in a way we would never dare in any other setting. And it culminates in an experience that the Bible says is "as strong as death" (Song 8:6). Theologians have suggested that because there is a total giving of the self in the sexual act, it is a kind of "little death."

Sexual love should come packed with devotion, but it is more than devotion. You can be devoted to a job or your softball team. Sexual love should be accompanied by wagonloads of friendship, but it is more than friendship. Sexual love should have intrinsic respect, but it is more than respect. You respect your parents. The uniqueness of physical love is what makes marriage a marriage.

The implications of comparing human lovers with the human being and God are many. If one accepts that this comparison/symbolism is valid, there are innumerable, rich correspondences to be made: the "mystery" of attraction, the power of the emotion, the openness (nakedness) and ecstasy, the natural ebb and flow of physical interest in relationships, the flirting and playfulness, and so on. Often it is *eros* that initially fuels the love interest between a man and a woman—it is our "first love." It is the moving power of pursuit, and by analogy, it represents the moving force of our faith expression. If a sexless marriage is dead, a passionless faith is dead too.

THIS CHANGES EVERYTHING

The idea of *eros* in faith challenges the view that faith is the rational brainchild of the human intellect. It means God dwells substantially in the soul. Faith is not a cold, austere, rationally based, anthropocentric (human) thing. It is a connection with and requires the participation of *Another.* This "otherliness" takes faith beyond one's personal internal experience, which means we are not just making stuff up in our heads.

When God told Moses to go into the wilderness, Moses answered, "If your Presence does not go with us, do not send us up from here" (Ex. 33:15). The real import of faith is not what we do *for* God, but what we do *with* Him. When Jesus commissioned His disciples to "Go and make disciples," He said, "And surely I am with you always, to the very end of the age" (Matt. 28:19–20). Christianity is not about what we do apart from God.

This was the problem with the disciples Jesus rebuked in the book of Revelation. Yes, they loved Jesus enough to "persevere" with devoted love. They had a rational, intellectual love in protecting the integrity of the Gospel—they "tested" teachers. Yes, they displayed sacrificial love—a love willing to lose for God. But they didn't seem to have a longing for the presence of God *Himself.* No "otherly" love—no *eros.*

How do you love God? Do you feel you are loving Him by maintaining doctrinal purity? That is good, but it isn't enough. Are you loving God by maintaining separation from the world and from sin? That is good, but it isn't enough either. How about being committed to reaching others for Christ and working hard in ministry? Daily devotions, following God's laws, and volunteering in church? All those things are good, but they are not enough. These kinds of love can be done without the direct presence of God. They are not "otherly" enough.

236

Jesus calls this "otherly" love "first love." Those of us who have fallen in love remember first-love feelings. The ones we loved captured our attention. They filled our minds. We anticipated their presence. We longed to be with them. It was definitely "otherly." Later we matured into devoted love, rational love, intellectual love, and sacrificial love. But those loves can be present in us when the one being loved is absent. Not so with first love. First love fights for the presence of the one being loved. Woe to us if we think mature love is enough. If we are not careful, mature love can quell "otherly," first love and harden the heart. We need to keep "otherly" love alive. We need to fight for first-love *eros*.

I think Jesus wants us to remember that faith is mostly about longing to be with Another. Our commitment to the disciplines needs to be all about connecting with the person of God—not the fulfilling of religious duty. We need to *find* God in prayer. We need to *find* Him at church. *Finding God* should be our focus when we skip a meal or pull into a season of silence. We need to be like the psalmist, who said, "My whole being follows hard after You and clings closely to You" (Ps. 63:8 AMP). We also need to be like Moses, who said, "Unless you go with us, we don't want to go" (Ex. 33:15, paraphrased).

It's so easy to make faith religious, or philosophical, or intellectual, or into some kind of inane belief. It only gets real and gritty when you pull aside into a secret, quiet place and lift your hands or get on your knees or lie on your face and begin to call out to God, to chase after Him. It gets real when you skip a meal, and as the hunger pangs dawn, you say, "I'm so hungry for You, God. My body is screaming for a Big Mac and fries. I can almost taste them. But I am more hungry for You than for physical food." This is *eros*.

This makes faith more than principles, doctrines, commitments, rule keeping, nobility, discipline, serving, integrity—things that can be done independent of the actual presence of God. In the real

Presence, things change. You think differently. You forgive more easily. You are more gracious, less self-pitying.

Ever hug a person doused with perfume? You carry her fragrance for a bit. The same thing happens when you spend time embracing God—you smell like God.

We carry His "fragrance" to a dying world (2 Cor. 2:14). We have been with *Another* and we are "otherly" in our demeanor.

Sadly, many assume the primary source of spirituality meaning and value lies in our own minds, how we think about God and reverence Him *in our own consciousness*. But the saints who have gone before us traced it back to deeper ground. They saw it as *transcendent*, or beyond the believer. It is bigger than us. God is in the mix of faith. The concept of *eros* is about being captured by a transcendent, bigger-than-us, "otherly" experience with the living God. It is precisely this "otherliness," this transcendent connection, that makes loving God so rich. It is the enterprise of "first loving" that protects us from the spiritual *hard heart*.

26

safe faith: in search of trust

When I first got into *God-loving*, I didn't really know much about what I was doing. Those first days were wonderful. There is something sweet and innocent about the moment you first believe. The writer of the song "Amazing Grace" said it this way: "How precious did that grace appear the hour I first believed."

God never intended that joyful first "hour" to be an explosion of hope and joy that faded into nothingness—like fireworks on the Fourth of July. Yet a good number of people, if they dare to be honest, would say that Christianity is less than they had hoped. At the very least, the milk has curdled; the soda has lost its fizz. What happened? We were supposed to *grow* in grace—to see increased fruitfulness. We were supposed to experience an ever-expanding sense of peace and joy. That was what we were told. But when grace looks better in the rearview mirror, something has gone wrong.

Then we begin to struggle with unsettling questions: *What's wrong with me? Did I do something that has made God angry with me? Maybe I am not doing enough.* So we try harder to do what we know is right, only to discover that a muscling faith isn't real faith. And the harder we try, the worse things get. The things that once gave us solace and encouragement lose their punch—we don't get as much out of prayer or study or going to church. Then darker thoughts begin to lurk in the back of our minds: *Maybe Christianity is just too hard for me to get,* or, *Maybe this isn't real after all.*

WHAT'S UP WITH US?

God gave us Eden, but we were so disobedient that He had to banish us to keep us from eating from the Tree of Life and thus living forever in a fallen state of shame. He gives us grace and forgiveness, and we flip it into crushing legalism. Grace is amazing, but so is the way we humans mess up what God gives us. It seems the best we can do is *bad.*

I think the basic problem in all of this is there is something in us humans that thinks we can replace God. That's the behind-the-scenes story with Adam and Eve. Satan told them, "If you eat of the forbidden, you will be *like God*" (Gen. 3:5, author's paraphrase). He was trying to sell them on the idea that if they became *like* Him, they wouldn't need Him. And they bought into it.

It's the "we won't need Him" part that has become the bane of the human condition—especially in the context of the Christian faith. We know our coming to Jesus was because of something God did (John 6:44); we can only grow in our faith because of the direct action of God (Heb. 12:2); we know from beginning to end that it's all about God—but like rabid dogs, we lunge to make faith about human effort and accomplishment. And therein lies the rub. When we make faith more about *us* than Jesus, religion goes bad. We stop celebrating our need for God and what *He* has done, and we start focusing on what *we* must do—as though we were God.

It took me a long time to understand what Jesus plainly said, "Apart from me you can do nothing" (John 15:5). Something in me thought I should be able to—if I were really worth anything (something in me still thinks that way). But I have become smart enough to realize it's a lie. The reality is, the best I can do on my own is mess things up.

As Christians, the problems start when we forget that salvation was always supposed to be *only* about Jesus Christ. We make it about Jesus *plus*. Jesus *plus* Bible study, Jesus *plus* not doing bad things, Jesus *plus* whatever we think we are supposed to do or not do. But it's never supposed to be Jesus *plus*; it's Jesus *alone*. When it is Jesus *alone*, the result is a changed life. Then we want to study; we want to *not* do bad things; we want to do what we are supposed to do.

It's a lot like falling in love. When you fall in love, you act differently. Seeing the work of God, His reckless love for us, His incautious forgiveness of all our failings, His faithfulness to take all the bad and the sour and work it into good, His plan to give us a future and a hope, *all* make us glow with love, adoration, and worship.

Human-centered religion isn't nearly so fruitful. When we are being religious, we are simply trying to get everything right and make it all fit. It's all about us, and we either live in the one ditch of failure or the other ditch of pride. We may mean well, but we still fall off the road.

Christianity is about God. Our faith is called "the Way" in the book of Acts (19:9). We are supposed to be loving our God on a road called life. When we get too religious, we are much more *in* the way than *on* the way. Hebrews 12:2 says, "Our faith comes from Him and He is the One Who makes it perfect" (NLV). Our job is trust Jesus to work out the perfection of our faith in God. If we don't, and we try to make our own faith perfect through man-made religious habits, we actually weaken our faith.

WE'RE OFF COURSE

As a pastor, people usually come to see me because something has gone wrong in their spiritual journey. They have lost their way.

241

Sometimes it is because of sin. Sometimes it's because of something that happened that confused or threw them off course. Often they ask questions like, "Why don't I feel anything anymore?" or, "Why is my faith so powerless?" or, "How did I start out so strong in my faith and end up so weak?"

With a few exceptions, all of them really love God. And all of them are really trying to please and serve Him—but that is also their problem. I have found that committed followers of Jesus, who have good prayer habits, disciplined Scripture study, and consistent church attendance, can end up with shipwrecked faith. And the harder they try to recapture their relationship with God, the worse it gets. Their human effort seems to cause their faith to be more compromised, tired, even diseased.

We understand disease. It robs the natural flow and function of the body. The body has natural defenses that fight diseases, but there are times when the body loses its capacity to ward off harm, and disease takes over. Unchecked, disease ravishes and destroys all the remaining health of the body. Similarly, I have found that good people get diseased faith, as I have illustrated in this book. Because people catch these "diseases" while doing religious things, perhaps now you can see why it seems appropriate to call them "religiously transmitted diseases" (RTDs).

Religion born from God's initiative is pure, undefiled, innocent, and powerful. Man-made religion looks a bit like the God-initiated kind (closely enough to fool many), but it is a *diseased* faith. And, sad to say, it is a disease that is easily transmitted to others. That's what this book has been about: *religiously transmitted diseases*. I've tried to give you a sampling of how we unearth faith from being rooted in God's graceful, unconditional gesture of love, and plant it, instead, in a repressive, prideful, often ill-motived human agenda that only produces sickness and death—*all the while thinking we are really serving God!*

242

Most believers I know, including myself, came to Jesus Christ with great appreciation and hope as we experienced His acceptance and forgiveness. We felt the wonder of coming to Him just as we were—not as what we promised to be. Unconditional love is to the human psyche what bright light is to a bug—we are drawn to it.

Though we long for unconditional love, our fallen brains default to thinking God is only offering it in order to initiate a relationship with us. But in order to establish an ongoing relationship, we convince ourselves that we must try to *do things* to keep His favor—to stay worthy of His love.

We consistently change faith from being about the wonder of God's initiative for relationship with us, *based on what Jesus Christ did*, to earning a relationship with Him, *based on what we do*. By doing so, we place the whole God–human connection on a different footing— the footing of human effort or man-made religion.

Though the RTDs may border on what we would characterize as sinful behavior, most of them are not overtly sinful. They are more like adding a pound of salt to a meat loaf recipe, instead of a teaspoon. It ruins the loaf experience. RTDs ruin the faith experience.

SAFE FAITH

It seems to me that the most difficult thing about Christianity is the whole *trust* piece—we are called to trust Jesus Christ—not just for salvation, but also for our daily lives. Trust, in the final analysis, is the only path that keeps faith *safe*. But that means we have to be comfortable with leaving control of things that directly impact our lives in the hands of *someone else*. If you have never had a good trust experience—where someone proved trustworthy, you will have a hard time with this. For many, only disappointment has followed trust—we even disappoint ourselves.

It is terrifying to think that we don't have the stuff to make it on our own. Something in us wants to believe that if we just *really* try, we can relieve the blunt reality of living in an imperfect and sometimes evil world. Instead of trusting in Another, we would rather trust that if we try harder, pray more, up our commitment to Christ, persevere, serve, surrender, and obey God more, life will adjust and we won't feel so bad—things are correctable, and *we* are the ones that can do something about it.

Trust, on the other hand, admits that we don't have what it takes to make it on our own and that we need help. There is something deeply disturbing about this position. It's like falling backward—instinctively we scramble for control. Something in us fights to prove we can control our lives. But the psalmist penned, "Man is a mere phantom as he goes to and fro: He bustles about, but only in vain"(Ps. 39:6). We may have our moments of resolve and confidence, but once we engage in the warp and woof of daily life, we discover that we do *not* have the wherewithal to win in life. The reality is, we are fallen. We are bankrupt. We need help outside of ourselves. But to *trust* instead of *try* feels a lot like suicide. Scary stuff.

There is a quiet terror that rises when we think we cannot control the ultimate outcome of our lives. So we foster the illusion that life spins out of control for those weak in faith, for those without knowledge, for those who don't give or pray much. And we create an illusion of control and busyness instead of a lifestyle of trust in the person of God, coupled with a longing for the return of Jesus. We are called into a surrendered relationship with the Lord Jesus Christ through every spiritual practice we can find (prayer, study, etc.), but we cannot trust in our performance of those spiritual practices (this is a little complicated to grasp, but it is a critical distinction).

Here is a silly analogy that may help: I just turned on the light switch in my family room. I didn't really think about the light switch and how important it was for me to walk up to the wall and throw that switch—I almost unconsciously flipped the switch in response to a need for light. My focus was on getting light into the room. I know that turning the switch *on* was critical in the process of getting light into the room, but turning on the switch didn't really create the light, nor did it *earn* the light. I have no ability to "light" anything. I need something outside myself to "light" my world. The flipping of switches is just my way of receiving help—it's a form of trust. That's what prayer and study and worship and all the spiritual things we do are to be—forms of trust.

There have been stormy nights, when the power went out and the light switch didn't work. I didn't think, *I better spend a couple of hours throwing the switch. Maybe I'm not doing it right.* Just as I am writing this, Gail walked into the room and flipped one of the other switches—the bulb popped and went dead (no kidding!). Maybe she needs to go to a seminar on how to turn on the switch more effectively? Or maybe the outcome was *outside of her control.*

There is no question that we have a role to play. Prayer, study, devotion, worship, and commitment are all important things. But they are the slenderest part of the deal. We should do them without trusting them. We should do them, trusting God. And if the light shines bright today, cool. If it's storming and there is no power, wait. God will get things up and running eventually. If the bulb pops, there needs to be some change. Bottom line, *we* are not the ones who can guarantee light. We can only throw the switch of faith (trust) and change some bulbs (repentance).

The people in the Bible, the saints throughout history, and our own lives prove that when we throw the switch, sometimes light comes, sometimes it's storming and the power is out, and sometimes our bulbs go dead. What do we do then? Our job it to trust and obey—not scramble for control.

But modern Christianity doesn't like trust. We want to believe that if we just increase our devotion time *or* give more money *or* claim the promises a little more tenaciously, the outcome can be determined by us. But at the end of the day, it's either got to be "praise God" or "praise my ability to get it right"—you can't have it both ways. I'm OK with living in the horror of "I will never get it right" and am running at every light switch I can find, yelling, "I need Your help, God!"

THE LAST WORD

There is a way to have a safe faith—where the joy, innocence, and purity of faith are not tainted. And it has everything to do with trusting Jesus. Jesus first; Jesus next; Jesus till the end. "That I may know him," was Paul's cry toward the end of his life (Phil. 3:10). May it always be ours. And may we always be free from religiously transmitted disease.

I hope this book has provoked you to fall back in love with Jesus. He is the secret to getting back to the joy of *the hour we first believed!*

notes

CHAPTER 5

Quote from C.S. Lewis at the University of London in 1944 entitled "The Inner Ring," http://oxfordalliance.blogspot.com/2005/11/inner-ring.html.

CHAPTER 6

1. Aristotle, *Nicomachean Ethics*, trans. Martin Ostwald. (New Jersey: Prentice Hall, 1999), para. 1180a: 29.
2. James A. Sanders, "Communities and Canon," *Oxford Study Bible* (New York: Oxford University Press, 1992), 91.

CHAPTER 8

1. Catherine Marshall LeSourd, *Something More* (New York: Inspiration Press, 1990), 191.

CHAPTER 10

1. David E. Roberts, *Existentialism and Religious Belief* (New York: Oxford University Press, 1959), 39.

CHAPTER 13

1. Oswald Chambers, *The Shadow of Agony* (Ft. Washington, PA: Christian Literature Crusade, 1934).

CHAPTER 15

1. C. S. Lewis, *Mere Christianity* (London: G. Bles, 1952), 190.

CHAPTER 17

1. Watchman Nee, *The Normal Christian Life* (Fort Washington: Christian Literature Crusade, 1961).
2. Paul Tournier, *Guilt and Grace* (New York: Harper and Row, 1959), 159.

CHAPTER 18

1. Packard, James I. *Knowing God.* (Downer's Grove, IL: InterVarsity Press, 1973).
2. Virginia Lively, *Healing in His Presence* (Grand Rapids, MI: Zondervan, 1984).

CHAPTER 23

1. Richard Wurmbrand, *Tortured For Christ* (Bartlesville, OK: Living Sacrifice Book Company,1967), 18–19.
2. Tony Campolo, *Speaking My Mind* (Nashville: W Publishing Group, 2004), 151.

CHAPTER 24

1. Charles Stanley, *Forgiveness* (Nashville: Oliver-Nelson Books, 1987).
2. Bill Hybels, *Who You Are When No One's Looking: Choosing Consistency, Resisting Compromise* (Downers Grove, IL: Intervarsity Press, 1987), 70–71.
3. Charles Stanley, *Forgiveness* (Nashville: Oliver-Nelson Books, 1987).

Want More?

 **Ed Gungor** has been in ministry for more than twenty years and is known for his practical and real communication. Ed and his wife, Gail, have four children and live in Tulsa, Oklahoma. Ed serves as Senior Pastor at Peoples Church and travels around the U.S. speaking in churches, universities, and conferences. To schedule an event or see Ed's speaking schedule, please visit edgungor.com.

If the message of this book has resonated with your heart, we'd love to hear from you and invite you to connect with us through our other resources. . . .

THE SALT VIDEO BLOG
A weekly email with a dash of video encouragement from Ed Gungor: www.theSalt.tv

PODCASTS AND WEB STREAMING
Available at our web sites

ALSO BY ED GUNGOR:

Getting Started: In Your New Life with Jesus

Tens of thousands of new believers have gotten off to a great start with this practical yet profound little book. Churches also purchase them as study guides to help people grow in their faith. Please visit our web site for ordering information and complete list of CD and DVD materials.

www.edgungor.com

LaVergne, TN USA
17 June 2010
186461LV00010B/3/A